Alfy

AN INCREDIBLE LIFE JOURNEY

AN INCREDIBLE
LIFE JOURNEY

Alfy Nathan

with

Joshua M. Sklare

Publisher: Montefiore Press

Editing and project management: Textbook Writers Associates, Inc.

Cover design: Julie Gallagher

Cover photo: Panoramic view of the Golan Heights, Sea of Galilee, Hula Valley and The Upper Galilee from Mount Hermon by Gal Forenberg

Text design and production: Gallagher

Printed in the United States of America

ISBN 978-0-9819265-0-6

The *Montefiore Press* is engaged in the writing, production and distribution of private books. Its sole purpose is to bring to light the stories of exceptional individuals who have made significant contributions in their professional, civic and philanthropic endeavors.

MONTEFIORE PRESS
Specialists in Private Books
www.montefiorepress.com

*It is true that most books come with
one dedication. But Alfy Nathan tends to
do things a bit differently. I have decided on
three seperate dedications.*

*The first dedication is to the founding
members of Kfar Hanassi.
There are many of you who have left this world,
but I shall never forget what we were able
to accomplish together. I am forever in
your debt for making my life interesting,
challenging, and meaningful.*

*My second dedication is to my 5 children,
15 grandchildren and 7 great grandchildren.
I am very proud of all of you and hope that
this book serves as a means for you to learn
about your rich history and heritage.*

*Lastly, I dedicate this book to my lovely wife Lil,
who has shared the joys and sorrows of these
past 34 years. Together we have travelled
what can only be described as an
"incredible life journey."*

CONTENTS

Contents

FOREWORD
by Laurie Kaye Glazer

I remember in the summer of 2002 climbing up the hill at *Nebi-Yusha* south of the Lebanese border in Northern Israel. With my husband Rob and our two sons, Andrew and Steven, and my mother by my side, Alfy led the way, acting as our tour guide. I had been to that very spot in 1980 with my sister Robin when Alfy had taken us on our first trip to Israel. My hope was that my children would benefit as much from the experience as we had. Nebi-Yusha had been the site of one of the most dramatic battles during the war for Israeli independence in 1948. Alfy escorted us up to the monument at the top of the hill. He was then 78 years old. He began to tell us the story of the battle that had taken place and we all became enthralled with his chilling and nostalgic tale. Alfy recognized many of the names on the monument and recalled the young men of the Palmach who were so young, yet so brave. As he relayed the story he became very choked up and this man of steel that I knew suddenly had tears in his eyes as he recalled the boys who had died at this site. It was one of the first times I remember seeing Alfy cry. It was then I began to discover the side of him that helped me to understand this proud, stubborn man and the world he left behind when he decided to move to America.

He was not an easy man to get to know, full of British mannerisms and fresh off the Israeli Kibbutz where he lived for nearly 30 years. Rough around the edges is putting it mildly. But now three decades later, he is one of the greatest men in my life and my sisters and I are blessed to have him for our father. There are five daughters in all and because of the tremendous and tireless efforts of Alfy and my mother, we are close. We don't live near each other. In fact we are spread out from California to Israel. But somehow we see each other several times a year. Every few years our parents manage to juggle schedule after schedule until the right date and the right place suits us all and off we go off on a family adventure—usually on a cruise ship, where none of us can escape. Their only rule is that we must have dinner together each night. And we do. And we love it. We have been to the Caribbean, Jamaica, Mexico, The Bahamas and Alaska. With their five daughters and spouses, we made a total of twelve. We always have a wonderful time, taking time to re-connect and creating new memories. My parents successfully molded a cohesive family unit from five eclectic daughters. We are truly blessed to have one another.

One trip in particular illustrates the incredible world Alfy and Lil created together. In the summer of 2008, our parents decided to coordinate a family cruise through Alaska. Only this time instead of 12 of us they decided it was time to invite the next generation of children—their 15 grandchildren, and their wives and/or significant others. 13 out of the 15 grandchildren were able to make it and there were a total of 31 family members on the ship. It was pretty incredible. We were celebrating two momentous occasions. Alfy had just turned 85 and it was our parent's 30th anniversary. The beautiful couple never looked prouder. When their eyes met, they seemed to be saying—"look what we have created." And they did. I think it amazes each and every one of us from the eldest daughter to the youngest grandchild that our family has grown so big and so close.

Writing about Alfy is no easy task. As his 5 daughters we ask, "Which Alfy are we speaking of?"

As a father, each of us can testify that he has been and continues to be there for us whenever we need him. He has helped us through the difficult times, and celebrated our joys. He has embraced each of our husbands, loving and accepting them as his own. He has been a role model, teaching us the value of giving, the beauty of acceptance and the pride that should come with being Jewish.

Foreword

As a grandfather to his 15 grandchildren, Alfy has shown a whole new generation what can be accomplished with vision and perseverance. He has taught them the value of family and the importance of family togetherness. Our parents take a genuine interest in and are totally devoted to each grandchild, taking every opportunity to spend time with them, talking about their dreams and aspirations. Every grandchild feels connected to them and in turn connected to each other.

As a husband, we can only say that together our parents truly exemplify what a loving and fulfilling marriage is all about. There is mutual respect, warmth and compassion, tenderness and affection and a strong devotion to family and family values. They are partners in life and support each other every step of the way.

Alfy is a dreamer and a visionary. His story reads like the mythical tale of a warrior hero with a dream to provide a safe haven for Jews and build up a country. He would risk his life to fulfill this dream and spend many years bringing it to fruition. His goal of becoming a successful entrepreneur was realized beyond even his wildest dreams and he is one of the most generous people we know and one of the most philanthropic. Alfy and Lil dreamed of building a life together and blending their two families into one. They are living their dream!

To us, Alfy is many things. He is a Kibbutznik, a traveler, an entrepreneur, a teacher, a leader and the patriarch of our great family and we are so proud to call him our father. He is one of a kind and the world is a much better place because of him. We are proud and excited to share his story.

INTRODUCTION

It has happened many times over the years. So many times, in fact, that I have begun to lose track. I find myself at some sort of an occasion, a benefit dinner or just a quiet evening together with some friends. I would start to talk about some of my experiences over the years. People would ask me questions about landing at Normandy or about the founding of the kibbutz.

Folks seemed to rather enjoy listening to my stories. Sometime during the evening the suggestion would be made that I commit some of these adventures to paper. Some went so far as to venture that the chapters of my life were exciting enough to form the basis of the chapters of a pretty interesting book. Nonetheless, for quite a number of years, I resisted such an undertaking.

While it is very flattering to hear compliments directed my way, I never thought of myself as being all that special. I just happened to be a guy in the right place at the right time. I just did what I could, what I felt I was supposed to do. Should I really write a book about it all? Well, my lovely wife Lil convinced me that I owed it to myself, my children, grandchildren, great-grandchildren, relatives, friends, and anyone else who may care to read about me to write the story of my life. I finally agreed.

There was just one problem; I did not know how to go about it. I came to the conclusion that I needed a collaborator. I have always believed that if you want a job done right, hire a professional. I began to search for one and was fortunate to meet Joshua Sklare, who seemed ideally suited to tell my story.

It seemed to me if Josh was going to gain an understanding of the forces that shaped my life, he should travel to the places where I lived and meet the folks that I shared my life with. He proceeded to do just that, interviewing folks on three continents and pouring himself into everything Alfy Nathan. Those he interviewed were not only very helpful but extremely gracious in receiving him. I am grateful to them all and will begin in England by thanking my sister Kit, her daughter Anne and son-in law, Arnold. My brother Sid, who sat together with them as they spoke of our childhood and a good deal more, deserves my thanks.

In Israel, I am likewise grateful to my brother Barry for all his help. From my days on the kibbutz, there were a good deal of folks who provided valuable insights. Special thanks are due to my long time friend Sheila Ben Yehuda who went above and beyond the call of duty in serving as a gracious hostess to Josh during his stay at Kfar Hanassi. Shmuel Hatzor, Eddy Niemenoff, and Rachel Ginat likewise have my thanks. Uri and Marga Goren of Rishon LeZion, who have been my friends for sixty four years were particularly helpful in matters dealing with my time in Marseilles. My daughter Rena, a neighbor of the Goren's in Rishon LeZion, has my sincerest thanks.

Back in the United States, I must extend my gratitude to my sister Mimi, who not only met with Josh but answered many of his subsequent inquiries. My daughters Yael, Sherry, Robin and Laurie all made significant contributions to this book, and they have my gratitude. My son-in-law Alex was particularly valuable in recollecting aspects of Sharon Pipping. Rena Olenick, whose own life story is a remarkable one, has my thanks. I am also grateful to my sister Sally for her input.

Though I have covered all of my siblings, I am not done with family yet. Rollie Abkowitz, my first cousin, is the person on my father's side whom we all look to for family details. She has been exceedingly generous in sharing valuable genealogical information. I am thanking her not only on behalf of myself but on behalf of generations yet to come. Thanks are also due my cousin Pauline Lubens for providing interesting details about the family. Brad Sargent of Living Legacies, an outstanding professional in his own right, was most helpful.

One of the lessons one learns in business is that success is achieved due to coordinated efforts of many people. I learned that the same thing holds true in turning out a book. Rose Sklare coordinated all of the steps that went along with producing this book. Julie Gallagher splendidly handled the composition and the layout of this book and is responsible for its handsome cover.

Lastly, I must thank my wife Lil for all of the time, effort and energy that she has expended on this book. She was a constant source of inspiration during the entire process. As much as this book has been a collaboration and a total group effort, whatever errors it may contain remain my sole responsibility. That being said, I hope the reader sits back, relaxes and enjoys the adventure that lies ahead.

Alfy Nathan
Northbrook, Illinois
April 2010

PART ONE

The Early Years

CHAPTER ONE

Call me Alfy

When you meet someone for the first time it is quite proper to ask the question "what name do you go by?" Especially when the person is a William or a Robert, and there are quite a number of possibilities. Sometimes that may change in the course of the person's life; he can be called one name as a boy, something else as a teenager, and so on, depending on the stage of life. For me the answer to this question has always been the same. My name has always been Alfy. I have always told everyone—no matter if it was a waitress in a restaurant, a business associate, or a new friend—to please call me Alfy. From childhood on, it has always been my preference, and many would say that it fits me like a pair of very comfortable shoes.

The name received some level of fame, particularly in my native England when Michael Caine made a movie about a London playboy named Alfie Elkins who had trouble settling down. It helped make Caine a big star. The refrain from the movie's soundtrack, "What's it all about Alfie?" seemed to be directed at me far too many times than I care to remember. Of course, if Michael Caine, exactly ten years and six weeks my junior and still very active, wants to play me in the movie version of this book, I would be very agreeable. But truth be told, Alfy is not my given name. I share my given name with a famous English prince and a chap named Einstein. But only my schoolmasters, with their sense of British propriety, insisted on calling me Albert. And what could I say to them. Certainly not "please call me Alfy!"

When I am called to the Torah in the synagogue, the name that is used is Avraham Ben Natan. Abraham, the son of Nathan. Avraham, my Hebrew name, is in memory of my uncle, my father's younger brother who died in childhood in Russia. They called the boy Avremele, an endearing take on Avraham. I have only seen pictures of this little boy wearing a cap and a cute smile, and apparently it was a custom to name children after uncles or aunts who died young and thus never had children of their own, so I am pleased to be able to perpetuate his memory.

I was born on 30 April 1923, in Wanstead, in the county of Essex in the southeast of England, my parent's country home. My folks, Harry Nathan and Anna Gurevitch Nathan, were both born in the old country, both from the Minsk area in Belorussia. My father had been born Nathan Hershkowitz, the son of Max Hershkowitz and Fruma Elka Bunin Hershkowitz. It could be that I get my sense of adventure at least partially from my grandfather Max Hershkowitz, who left Minsk in the latter part of the 19th century to work in South Africa. I know not why he went or what he did there, but apparently, my father, who was the oldest of six children, decided to join him there. He made his way to London, where he intended to catch a steamer bound for the Cape. But as luck would have it, what they call the Second Boer War broke out and interfered with his plans. He was stuck in London and made his way there as a peddler. He wanted to stay permanently in his new country, but after my grandfather returned from South Africa, he summoned my father back to Russia. But my father was destined to return to England because after a few years, his famous cousin, Lev Bronstein, better known to us as Leon Trotsky, was arrested and sent to Siberia. The rest of the family was terribly worried that the Czarist secret police would start arresting all Lev's known friends and relatives, and so that was all the reason my father needed to return to London.

The Hershkowitz Family: Grandmother Frume Elke,
Grandfather Max, Aunt Dora, and Ida, taken in New York City
(Photo courtesy of Rollie Abkowitz)

Upon his return my father decided to change his name. He went from Nathan Hershkowitz to Harry Nathan. It sounded more English, yet he was not trying to hide the fact he was Jewish. My father was tremendously proud of his heritage and he instilled that feeling in his seven children. I was the fifth to come along. My oldest sister was Cissy, and next there was Sally, then Kit, and finally my brother Sid, and after I came along in '23, there was my sister Mimi, and then my baby brother Barry. Quite a large brood, and as you will see throughout the course of this book, we are a close knit bunch.

My parents met through my dad's friend, Kahlman Gurevitch. Uncle Kahlman was talking to my dad one day when he mentioned that he was going to pick up his family who were just arriving from the old country. He asked my father if he wanted to tag along. He agreed, and as the family finished being processed by the authorities my father caught a glimpse of Kahlman's sister, a young woman named Anna. He was smitten, and after a courtship, they got married. It was a good *shidduch* (match). The families knew one another from the old country and it is possible they were even distantly related.

All of my relatives were glad to be out of Russia, where it was hard economically and the threat of pogroms was ever present. My father's family left Russia around the same time, but they did not come to London. They went to America, where the streets were paved with gold, arriving and settling in New York City. They had asked my father to join them in America, but he was already becoming well established in business and so remained in England. In those days, there were no cell phones or phones of any kind; keeping in touch was done by handwritten letters mailed at the post office and not by e-mails typed on the computer. They stayed in touch, and my father was keenly aware of the goings on with his siblings, but it would be years before he would see his sisters and their families in what must have been quite a reunion. But now I am getting ahead of myself.

The fact that I was born in a country home should tell you that my father had managed to do well. Like many Jews, he had started as a peddler and graduated to storekeeper. At the peak of his considerable success, H. Nathan had eight stores. That is not to say we were Rothschilds, or even close to being in that class, but we managed to live quite comfortably. H. Nathan stores all carried a complete assortment of men's and women's clothing (with the exception of men's suits) linens, towels, draperies, and other household items.

The original H. Nathan store, what today we would call our flagship store, was located in the Stratford section of London, and the customers were all working class folks. Every shilling they earned working in factories and in the rail yard counted, and they had to be judicious in the way they bought what we sold, or else they would not have enough for food or rent. For really big purchases they would use Lay-by or Layaway, meaning they would put aside a certain amount from their paycheck every week and put it toward the purchase. Sometimes it took several months or more until they had completely paid it off, but only then did they take the item home. It is the opposite of credit but it makes a lot of sense, and in this way people avoided serious financial trouble with escalating debt.

The family had originally resided in the East End, the center of Jewish life in London. But my mother, who in addition to raising us, took a very active role in running the store, found that the commute to Stratford was taking too much of a toll on her and taking time away from her dual role in the home and the business. She suggested to my father that we move closer to the store, and when a building became vacant next to the store, we purchased it. Our home was now directly above the store, cutting down considerably on the commute. Ours was a fine home, with eight bedrooms and fine furniture. The kitchen, with a bunch of growing children, was a pretty popular spot, and it had not one stove but two.

My mother had plenty of help, with both a nanny and a cook in her employ. Our cook was named Hetty, who was very much a member of our family. She was with us for many years and was very knowledgeable about how to maintain a kosher home. My mother had

serious. When afternoon rolled around, she would stand and pray the *mincha* (afternoon) service. Sometimes she would spend the entire Sabbath with us. My mother would put the dry, cooked food on the *blech* (tin metal pan placed over the stovetop, where a low flame continues burning during the Sabbath when cooking is not allowed) for the Sabbath lunch but my *Bubbe* did not approve of this. She would instead only eat cold food for the Sabbath lunch, and I remember her eating her sandwich. She was not a woman given to change, and despite her small stature, cast a very large shadow indeed. I think that whatever her feelings at the time and wherever she is looking down on us today, she must be rather proud. For whatever we are, we are all proud Jews who have kept the religious traditions we were raised on to the best of our abilities.

My mother used our fairly large home to great advantage in a variety of ways. Often many items were stored in the house waiting to be auctioned off at a JNF (Jewish National Fund: an organization that raised funds to buy land in Palestine for Jewish settlement) bazaar. It was not uncommon for local Jewish brides to use the large sitting room to hold a bridal shower: people would come there to give gifts for the young bride to use to outfit her new home. We actually called the sitting room the backroom, and the young ladies who used the room for such purposes were known as "backroom brides." They were obviously very grateful for the opportunity to use the space. While such a thing would be rare today, most people lived in small places then, and there were not a lot of halls or storage available in London for such things.

This reflects the strong feeling of community we were raised with, and the idea of helping people came naturally for my parents. And if you learned to defer in matters regarding the house for the sake of community and charity, you learned to sacrifice a bit when the Jewish holidays rolled around. How could I forget the several days right before Passover? In addition to all the general excitement, the bathtub was converted into an aquarium where a few large carp would swim around in their cramped quarters and patiently wait their turn to become gefilte fish.

While we had great meals for the holidays and my sisters would frequently get new clothing to wear, the holidays were not the only special times for our family. We had a very special evening together each and every week. The Friday night Shabbat dinner was a major event in our family life. It was more than just a dinner. Of course the food my mother and Hetty prepared included all the usual Sabbath delicacies. Looking back on it, it is not the taste of the gefilte fish, chicken soup, or tzimmes that I most remember, though I surely savored these dishes. It was the family spirit, the special feeling of togetherness that pervaded the table. Because there were seven of us children, it was the one time of the week that everyone gathered together. We learned to appreciate the blessing of family at those Shabbat meals. When I came to America in 1976, one of the first things that struck me was that many families did not gather together at the dinner table on Friday night. Instead, it seemed to be more like a sports night where the kids would play on their school or local teams. I always felt they were missing out on something. I remain grateful for the Friday nights of my childhood.

Our family was very active in the rather Gentile sounding West Ham Synagogue on Earlham Grove Street in Forest Gate. The shul (synagogue) that was closest to our home, attracted people from all over the area. Many lived one or two miles away. Like my parents, the majority of congregants were from Eastern Europe, from places like Minsk, Warsaw, and Vilna. Many, if not most, were shopkeepers like my parents. On Saturday morning, all of us kids would trot off to the synagogue to attend services. Our observance of the Sabbath laws did not permit us to drive, so we would all walk to the synagogue, something I actually rather enjoyed. Festivals such as Passover and *Shavvot* (Feast of Weeks) attracted larger crowds than the typical Sabbath, partially because they recited the *Yizkor* (remembrance prayers for the departed) service, which were particularly special occasions. I enjoyed listening to the cantor chant the prayers and as this was England, everything was even more formal than what one would see in the United States.

On the High Holy Days, there would be such a huge throng of people that there would be an overflow service where, in addition to our rabbi and cantor, an important rabbi and scholar, usually a member of the London *Beth Din* (religious court), would speak to us. During this the entire congregation would remain silent. If someone did talk, one of the ushers would yell out "*Sha*." Yom Kippur (the Day of Atonement) was serious business. In the years before my Bar Mitzvah, I would fast a little longer each day to get used to the feeling of going without food and water. But by the time I was thirteen and knew that I would not be eating for quite a while, I felt a bit weak. When after the *Musaf* (Additional) prayers were over and the intermission began and I began the long trek home, not only was my stomach aching from hunger, but my feet were really tired from all the standing during the service. I played a little game to make the walk easier. I would count seven trees as I walked along, and then rest for a few minutes, then count the next seven trees. After all, seven is a lucky number, and eventually I made it home.

Our family was very active at the synagogue. My father served for a while on the Board of Management (similar to the Board of Directors here in the States), and all my siblings attended the *Cheder*, which is what many today call Hebrew School. Several of us sang in the children's choir and attended Habonim (the Labor Zionist youth movement, which I will have a good deal to say about later) that met there. We seemed to be in that building all the time, but unlike a lot of youngsters today, we never complained. We took to all of this. Of course, my brother Sid and I did run into a little bit of trouble with Mr. Barnett, our *Cheder* teacher. While most of the *melamdim* (teachers) were from the old country, Mr. Barnett was as British as afternoon tea. He was, as my brother Sid once poignantly described, "a very, very severe man," and this may have been because of his daytime job as an English schoolmaster.

We were just regular kids, and having already gone to our regular school during the day, had the need or at least the urge to let loose a bit. (My grandchildren and great grandchildren will be gratified to know that some things change very little over generations, kids will be kids.) Sid was mistakenly blamed for some ruckus that had occurred in the classroom, and Mr. Barnett had taken this up with my father. Then, I ran afoul of the authorities when restlessness, no doubt fueled by afternoon hunger, led me to climb on top of the Shul's *Sukkah* (booth or hut built by the synagogue to be used during the Feast of Tabernacles) and picked off one of the apples placed there for decorative purposes—it seemed perfectly edible to me. Mr. Barnett did not see it as a harmless prank and brought my indiscretion to the attention of my father.

Perhaps I had a taste for mischief, but it all turned out well in the end. My father thought that the best solution to the problem was for me to join my brother Sid and take private lessons with Rabbi Lipshutz. Rabbi Lipshutz was a wonderful man, an old European fellow with a long white beard and a friendly smile. We would travel on the tram to the East End, where his flat doubled as our classroom. The location of the flat was well known to us since it was adjacent to the Jewish Lads Brigade, a quasi-military youth organization founded by Colonel Albert Edward Goldsmid, a war hero from the Boer War and an early Zionist whom we admired a good deal. Rabbi Lipshutz always made us feel very comfortable, not like the stodgy schoolmaster, Mr. Barnett. He would serve us tea in a glass and then give us a sugar cube, which we would place between our teeth to enhance the sweetness. I remember the old snuff box he kept by his side, a dark brown wooden ornament with some kind of engraving etched into the sides that I could never quite make out. The box held the dry tobacco or snuff he sniffed into his nostrils for a little pick-me-up. He would then

Seated in a fancy wooden chair with my brother Sid by my side.
Notice how dapper we looked wearing suits, caps, and neckties.

stroke his beard and teach us how to read properly from the *Chumash* (Bible) with the famous medieval rabbinic commentary of *Rashi*.

But what was best of all, and as sweet as the tea that we drank, were the stories from the Bible that he told us. They came alive for me. Of the young David and the mighty Goliath, so you felt as if you were there when the slingshot felled the Philistine warrior. And the climatic meeting between Jacob and Esau, when you were unsure if Jacob would escape the wrath of his jealous brother. Speaking of jealousy, nothing quite got to me as when Rabbi Lipshutz would speak of Joseph being sold in slavery by his brothers. You could feel the agony of being thrown into a pit and later in jail, and then the joy when he was released from jail and appointed Viceroy of Egypt and eventually reunited with his brothers. It was like watching a movie—you wanted to warn Joseph before he spoke to his brothers and then you wanted to keep quiet and not let on, when the brothers came to Egypt when there was a famine in the land of Israel and they appeared before their brother Joseph. Fortunately, it worked out well in the end. And I developed an early appreciation for the geography of many of those amazing stories; those famous places in the Land of Israel that I would eventually discover for myself when I set foot on the Holy Land's ancient soil.

Though I have been a lifetime reader, an activity that has given me joy and satisfaction over the years, I did not particularly distinguish myself scholastically when I was young. I always loved working with my hands and eventually chose a technical track rather than an academic one. But school was not the only place to learn things. I received quite a practical education working at the family store. It seemed as if we all started working at the store about as soon as we learned to walk. Even my brother Barry, who was just a baby, could be found at the store, and one of us would watch him as he rested in the pram. The store, which was relatively small by today's retail standards, used every available square inch for selling space. And that included not just the inside of H. Nathan. We maintained a pushcart on the outside where we hawked our least expensive goods. It was my first experience selling, and I did pretty well at it. I also got my first taste of dealing with customers. Many of the products on the pushcart were manufactured in Japan, and if "Made in Japan" at the time was synonymous with cheap goods, these items certainly were. The men's socks sold for 2 ½ pennies apiece and five pairs for a shilling. These were socks for working men, and they would wear them a number of times until they wore out rather than darning them; our customers would just toss them out and buy new ones.

Like most children, the time came when I wanted to get a bicycle. My father told me that I would have to contribute a certain amount toward the purchase price. Though I did not realize it at the time, he was doing me a favor by making me work for something I wanted. To earn extra money, I expanded my business activities beyond my work at the store. I noticed that in the days and weeks before Passover, housewives would flock to the Jewish stores to buy all the required food and wine for the holiday. These women would have to drag these items home, and it was there that I sensed an opportunity. I rented a pushcart, and would offer to take the items to their flats for a small fee, of course. It was a seasonal business to be sure, but I did quite well with this every year and managed a few similar ventures. I must have liked being an entrepreneur, because I would return to being my own boss over 40 years later.

It was not a childhood filled only with school, work, and chores. There was fun and adventure as well. Some of the greatest times were the trips we took to Epping Forest. It was summertime, and my father would get up early in the morning to pack some of us lucky kids into the motor car. He would tie his bicycle on top of the hood, and off we would go. He would park on one of the side roads and cycle back to Stratford to open the store for business, and then return at the end of the day to pick us up. Epping was called "the People's Forest" because it was maintained for the recreation of Londoners—and it was just that. There were all manner of places to explore and run around in, and as you can guess, there were no worries about crime or anything of the sort in those days. We were good and tired by the time evening rolled around.

The only thing that may be more closely associated with England than tea time is fish and chips. If you ever read Dickens, you may remember a famous line in *The Tale of Two Cities*, "Husky chips of potatoes fried with some reluctant drops of oil." And the oil was not always so reluctant. Of course, that was only half of this magnificent combination. The other half, the fish part, was usually made either from haddock or cod, both extremely abundant throughout England at the time. So popular were fish and chips that it seemed as if there were fish and chip shops on every corner, like hamburger joints in Chicago or falafel stands in Tel Aviv. Sometimes I would go with my brother to Jack's Fish and Chips place in another neighborhood. But my favorite place was Mr. Cohen's fish market, located near our family store. Mr. Cohen, who was one of the Jewish merchants in our neighborhood, was very active in our synagogue and friendly with my father. I still remember the funny looking clock in his shop. What made it unusual is that he had taken off the hands, rendering it virtually useless. Why, you ask, would Mr. Cohen do such a thing? Very simply, he tired of people coming in off the street to get a glimpse of the clock. After all, he must have thought, I am in the fish business and not in the business of providing updates on the time.

Well, sell fish he did, specifically fresh fish in one part of the store and in the other corner he had his fryer going full blast. I would watch him dip the fish in flour and eggs and then fry it until it was good and crisp. The final touch was to sprinkle the fish liberally with salt and vinegar. The potatoes were similar to American french fries, only much better, and they would be cooking in the other frying pan. When it was all done, he would wrap the concoction in grease proof newspaper, and then you could eat it, or rather devour it on the spot. Best of all, it was cheap and Sid and I used to love to go down to Cohen's every chance we got. Later, one of our cousins owned several fish and chips places, and after he sold them, he became an expert business broker who specialized in the purchase and sale of fish and chip shops. Though English cuisine often gets a bad rap for those who do not appreciate kidney pie or Yorkshire pudding, despite all my years in Israel and America, I still miss the fish and chips. The smell of it when I return home to England brings back so many childhood memories. And though the Empire is no more, the British still have fish and chips, a small vestige of what was once the best food when you are good and hungry.

Many Jews from Eastern Europe were either afraid of dogs or reluctant to own them. Not so my father. He loved dogs and he became the proud owner of a good number of greyhounds. Although the breed had originally been trained as hunting dogs, this soon changed. Their great speed made them excellent racing dogs. And boy, could they move. I used to spend time at the kennel where we kept the dogs. I would take them out for a walk, play with them, and naturally, they took to me as much as I did to them. Some of them were big winners on the track, some not so successful. But it did not matter to me. I loved them just the same. Of course, I did get a particular thrill when one would win a major race and my father received the prized trophy cup. It was a gold or silver ornament that could be proudly displayed. We would hold it up high, and the best part for me was that I would get to accompany the dog around the track, as the roar of the crowd acknowledged our champion canine and us, the proud owners.

Chilblains are, thankfully, very rare these days. Most prevalent during the winter season, this malady involves a swelling and reddening of the fingers and toes and can make a person very, very uncomfortable. I should know, for when I was young I contracted a really bad case of it. My fingers were as bloated as sausages and they turned salami red. But as much as they hurt me, I think my older sisters were even more upset by the condition than I was. Kit was practically in tears when we spoke about it not long ago. There was not much to do except wait for winter to finally abate and the temperature to rise a bit. Nevertheless, everyone did try to relieve my suffering. Hetty would cover me in blankets, and using ointments and some homemade remedies, would do her best to alleviate the swelling.

Since there was a significant age difference in our family, my older sisters began to get married while I was still in my formative years. Cissy was the oldest, and when she became engaged to a young man, my father wanted to help the young couple start out, so he purchased for his prospective son-in-law a fruit and vegetable store, or what was called a "green grocer" in England. It was a very fine thing to do, but the engagement was broken, and my dad was then stuck with a fruit and vegetable store. So although he was very busy with his own retail operation, he ran the store for a time until he was able to sell it. We all helped out there, too, but what I remember is how much I enjoyed waking up in the morning, at an hour that can only be described as ridiculously early, and going to the commercial area where the wholesalers operated to watch my father negotiate with them. We would then take the produce back to our store and sell it to our customers. Of course, I might end up with some tasty fruit for my efforts.

I should add that everything worked out well in the end for Cissy, as she later met the man she did marry, Alex Brooks, and my father helped set them up in renting out rooms in a boarding house. They started out with a six room boarding house, and through hard work ended up owning and operating a very large hotel. The same happened to my sister Kit, who married Dave Solomon. My father helped them get started in the hairdressing business, and from one shop they expanded to successfully running a number of them, a business continued by their daughter and son-in-law.

CHAPTER TWO

Depression and Tragedy

The stock market crash in New York happened in 1929, when I was only six years old. But the repercussions of a worldwide depression were felt throughout most of the thirties. Naturally, the family stores were severely affected by the massive unemployment that ensued. The streets of Stratford, normally bustling with sounds of commercial activity, were more than a few decibels quieter during this period. We lived on a main street, one normally full of pushcarts and stores. Some were forced to shut down. Not long ago my sister Kit reminded me that during the good times one of the loudest sounds to be heard was that of metal banging against the cobblestones. These came from the iron bits attached to the work boots, reinforcing them so they would last longer. The thumping sound could be heard as the men got off the buses and trams and began their walk to the large railway yard that assembled train engines. The thumping noise could be heard up to 8:00 A.M., when the whistle blew and they began work. At half past twelve, the whistle would blow again for lunch, and the thumping sound would begin anew, stopping when the whistle blew to signify that lunch was over. At 5 P.M. the whistle blew again, the day was done and the clumping could be heard anew. Eventually the railway yard closed down. The loud thumping noises ceased, and the new sound was the idle chatter of the men as they stood around the street corner, with despair in their eyes.

There is nothing worse than men with nothing to do, with only time on their hands. I suppose there is something to the famous saying that "idle hands are the devil's workshop." And all manner of fads, such as marathon dancing and flag pole squatting or sitting, which had taken root during the twenties, became very popular during the depression. People were looking for any diversion from their personal troubles and actively embraced anything that would do the trick. In fact, there was a famous one held at the Forest Gate Rink in the winter of 1932. For the poor bloke, or human limpet, as they used to jokingly refer to people who engaged in this activity, the grand prize was all of 10 pounds, which to a man without a job is a lot of money. Though it sounds ridiculous today to sit and watch people sit on poles for hours on end, that is precisely what people did. Of course, this was for sport as the one who remained the longest won a prize, and no doubt there were some side bets placed among some in the crowd. For the winner, it was a way to earn some money, and for all the spectators, a carnival-type spectacle or as some called it, a "freak show," was preferable to facing the reality of the times. That is, until the spectacle finally ended. Sooner or later everyone goes home and reality sets in again like a recurring bad dream. Or so it seemed in those dark economic days.

Besides pole sitting, the primary diversion in West Ham had always been, like most English cities, its football team. Though we lived not far from the Royal Theatre, it could never really compete culturally with football for the hearts of most of the neighborhood people. For my American friends and relatives, English football is what you folks refer to as soccer in the U.S. Our local team was called West Ham United, and as the famous headline of a local newspaper once proclaimed of its most famous former player and manager, Syd King, "West Ham is Syd King." Most of the locals felt that way. Syd King was the local hero, a larger than life figure, a handsome and debonair type who loved strong drink and pretty women, and not necessarily in that order. He was a true king to much of the faithful. And the locals in the pub, of which West Ham had plenty, loved to talk about King and the team, which enjoyed considerable success throughout my boyhood. Unfortunately, during that depression year of 1932, the team faltered and there were rumors of financial impropriety on the part of King. He was suspended and later fired as a result. So devastated was Mr. King that he committed suicide shortly thereafter, but West Ham United played on, the hopes of many of the workingmen of the area resting on the results of their matches at what we called Boleyn Castle, the local stadium. This stadium was somehow connected to Anne Boleyn, the second wife of good old Henry the Eighth, though I seem to have forgotten the specific details.

Fortunately, our family managed to hang in there despite the rough economic times. My father was a shrewd businessman and did his best to adapt to the worsening conditions. We all stuck together. But the worldwide depression paled alongside the disaster about to descend on our family. It would hit us with all the subtlety of a tidal wave. The year was 1934. My mother went into the hospital for what was supposedly a routine procedure. She was to have the operation, recuperate in the hospital, and then come home completely cured. She should have been fine, but she never made it home. I was a lad of eleven and all I remember is standing by the staircase when I began to hear frantic cries from my older siblings as my father told them my mother had died. The wailing went on, and I could feel myself shivering uncontrollably, much worse than chilblains. And it would not stop. I felt my heart beating hard and my stomach begin to turn. I had never felt anything like this agony. My three older sisters were always very strong people. I had never seen them like this, but much as they were hurting, they always looked out for their younger brothers and sisters, for Sid and Mimi, baby Barry, and of course, me. They helped comfort us, hugging us tightly and reassuring us that all would be okay.

We buried my mother in an old fashioned type of Eastern European funeral. Our family had the collars and lapels of our shirts and jackets ripped in a dramatic way, in what is known as *Kriah,* the traditional rending of the garment. Not only was our family crying, but there were old ladies, many of whom did not know my mother, who attended all Jewish funerals and whose job was to cry loudly and emotionally and therefore stir up feelings in everyone present. The rabbi gave a eulogy, extolling all my mother's virtues, and then the cantor sang the prayer for the dead and the men said the mourner's *kaddish.* We then went back to our home for a meal in which I remember eating a hardboiled egg and other similarly shaped foods supposed to symbolize that life is like a circle. Tragically, my mother's had been a small circle as she was taken so young.

People came to visit during the seven days of the *shiva,* and we all sat on a low chair or stool. The mirrors were covered. But the house seemed eerily empty without my mother. And it was never again the same. Of course, we all wondered why my mother had died while having routine surgery. There was an official inquest, and because I was so young I did not understand all of what was going on. In time I learned more about it. We all suspected negligence on the part of the hospital but never got the full story. It would remain a mystery, and many of us thought that the hospital administration covered up what happened to protect themselves. I am sure the secrecy surrounding the whole matter partly reflected the times and the lack of transparency in such things. Not that learning the truth would make the loss any easier, but it is bad to be left with a mystery, for it tends to linger and fester inside.

We all tried our best to put a brave face on our new circumstances, but it was very difficult. I would accompany my brother Sid, who had already had his Bar Mitzvah, to the synagogue to say the mourner's *kaddish.* Although we were always close, I suspect that the tragedy made us even closer. It was also very tough for my dad, as he was alone for the first time in years. Many men remarry as soon as it is permissible to do so, while others seem to stay in a state of permanent mourning or remarry only many years later. My father remarried soon afterwards, and this proved very difficult for the family, particularly my older sisters. It just did not sit well with them. They were pretty much all adults, and either already on their own or ready to be so, and my father's remarriage may have hastened their move out. Years later, after my father eventually divorced his second wife, everyone reconciled. But every family has its challenges, its difficulties, and its misgivings about things that could have been handled better. Of course, hindsight is always 20/20.

As for my own Bar Mitzvah, I remember little of it for a very good reason. My mother's death had pierced my heart so I was in no mood to embrace what should have been a joyous occasion. My performance, reading the Haftorah, having my first *aliyah,* and giving a brief speech about the weekly Torah portion, could best be described as perfunctory. My childhood innocence had largely ended with my mother's death, and it would take some time for the boyish grin to return to my face. But thank God, it did eventually return. And in that sense, it was a lesson that pain can be endured, and that everyone, no matter what the pain or loss, has the ability to go on and have a happy life.

Such an experience also brings with it the realization that no matter how much you are hurting in life, some people have a much tougher time. Some have circumstances far more challenging than the Nathan family. One such example was the Asher family. I mentioned that the men who worked in the railway yards wore boots reinforced with iron bits that made clanging sounds when banged against cobblestone streets. It was this particular sound, and its cadence, like that of an army marching, which signaled the economic vitality of London's industry.

Well, there is a story behind the iron bits. Charles Asher was a cobbler who owned a shoe store in the area. After World War One, he discovered that thousands and thousands of army boots that had been manufactured to serve the troops would no longer be needed and could be had, like most military surplus, for a very good price. He proceeded to purchase as many as he could afford, and then by adding the metal bits and otherwise reinforcing the boot, he converted it into a working boot, ideal for the men working in heavy industry. He did very well, but sometime in the 1920s, he died. He left a widow with seven children. My sisters were friendly with some of the girls in the family, and Kit and Sally kept in touch with them for years. I think only one is alive now. As you can imagine, they struggled mightily, and Mrs. Asher could barely feed her family. Finally one day Mr. Livermore knocked at our door. He had a fish store in the neighborhood where he primarily sold shellfish, and as such was a kind of Gentile Mr. Cohen. He told my father that he lived next door to the Asher family and described some of their struggles. As Pesach was coming up, this man was worried that Mrs. Asher would not be able to purchase the food necessary for the holiday. He told my father that whatever money my father could raise from his friends, Mr. Livermore would match the amount. Mr. Livermore was a truly amazing and generous man. The prawns he sold may not have been kosher but his heart was. He was concerned about the plight of a Jewish widow, just as in the story of Naomi in the Book of Ruth. And although Rabbi Liphshutz had taught me that responsibility for providing for those in need is incumbent on the community, what we call *Maot Chitim*, sometimes it takes a Gentile to remind us what is expected. And the best medicine against feeling sorry for yourself and your family is to help others.

One of the results of the tragedy is that all of the siblings became very close, perhaps closer than if we had not had to endure such a loss. I guess we realized that all we really had was each other, and despite the fact that we are all strong people and individualistic to the core, there resides within each of us a sense of togetherness that is not found in all families. One of my siblings summed up the spirit best when she said, "When one of us bleeds, we all feel it." Ours is a bond that can never be broken, and as the remaining six of us live in four different countries on three separate continents, we have a bond that forms a

In England with my siblings at a family celebration. Left to right:
Mimi, me, Kit, Barry, Sally, and Sid. Sadly, Cissy had already passed on.

chain that stretches across land, water, and time zones. It is a bond
that developed in childhood, but was made unbreakable through the
tragedy that was the loss of our mother. It can only be broken in death,
but I hope we all have many more years to enjoy each other. But now I
am getting sentimental and worse, I am getting ahead of myself.

CHAPTER THREE

The Farm and the Battle of Cable Street

Like many British Jews of the era, my family was strongly Zionist. And in Britain, which controlled Palestine through the British Mandate, feelings ran high. The hopes and aspirations for a Jewish homeland in Palestine were raised significantly on November 2, 1917, when Lord Rothschild received a letter from Arthur James Balfour, then serving as Foreign Secretary. That letter, which consisted of only one very long sentence, read:

> *His Majesty's Government view with favour the establishment in Palestine of a national home for the Jewish people, and will use the best endeavours to facilitate the achievement of this object, it being clearly understood that nothing shall be done which may prejudice the civil and religious rights of existing non-Jewish communities in Palestine, or the rights and political status enjoyed by Jews in any other country.*

The Balfour Declaration, with its measured, carefully calibrated language, raised hopes, but these hopes were slow to be realized. So slow was the progress that my sister Mimi tells the story of when our father took her to the cinema to see a movie that strongly advocated for a Jewish state. It was sometime in the late 1930s and Mimi quoted our father's reaction, "It may not happen in my lifetime, it may not happen in your lifetime. But someday, we will have a country of our own." That it was to happen so much sooner than my father expected and in his lifetime is part of the story of this book, but before I digress too much let me tell you how I became interested in being a Zionist.

Zionist youth groups became very strong in the 1930s. In the case of our family, we became very active in Habonim, the youth movement of Labor Zionism. It was the strongest of all the different factions in England which included the Religious Zionists, Revisionists, and *Hashomer Hatzir*. Of course, one of the reasons that Zionist youth movements were so popular at the time was the general rise in youth movements of all types throughout Europe. Walter Laqueur, the prominent Jewish historian, commented on the reasons behind this powerful trend when he said,

At a time when family ties were loosening, when protest against school and other forms of authority was spreading, these youth movements provided new ideals and values, the promise of both national revival and a new and better way of life. In common activities, such as discussions, seminars, sports meetings, camping and excursions, a spirit of community was developed. The members taught Hebrew and the essentials of Jewish history and culture. They regarded Palestine, and specifically in the collective settlements, not just as part of the solution of the Jewish question, long overdue, but as the most desirable way of life for idealistic young men and women. In this respect the Zionist youth movements of the day, which in the European dictatorships simply served as a reserve army to replenish the ranks of the state party, or as in the democracies, failed to carry the idea of a live community beyond the dreams of adolescence.

The Farm and the Battle of Cable Street

Just about all my brothers and sisters attended Habonim meetings, which were held weekly at our synagogue. That fact alone shows how nicely Zionism fit in with traditional Judaism. Habonim itself was a little like fish and chips in that it was thoroughly British. And though like fish and chips it would spread to many other Western countries, its center would always remain in England. What was to become Habonim grew out of a series of lectures about Jewish culture given by Wellsley Aaron in 1928. From there it grew quickly, and I started going to meetings at the beginning of my teenage years, soon after my mother died. I immediately fell in love with Habonim. It was to become a serious love affair, one that continues to this day as I still read the organization's magazine, *Kol Vatikei Habonim*, with great interest.

Part of the focus of Habonim was educational, as we learned about the ideology of both Zionism and socialism. We learned about the great thinkers and leaders of Labor Zionism such as Nachman Syrkin, Ber Borchov, A. D. Gordon. It was all about the melding of two ideologies, Zionism and socialism, and so fused were they that when someone once asked me how much of Habonim was Zionism and how much was socialism, I answered that it was impossible to answer since the two were inseparable from one another.

Chaim Weizmann

The man I admired most as a Zionist leader was not a Labor Zionist at all but a General Zionist, Chaim Weizmann. Weizmann was born in Eastern Europe. He was a chemist and Zionist leader who headed the British Admiralty Laboratories during the First World War and developed a new process of producing acetone. He was a major force behind the Balfour Declaration, but what I admired most about Weizmann was not his

On David Elder Farm. I am riding one tractor, Johnny Tena is
behind me on the second tractor.

significant academic achievements but his practical, action oriented
approach to Zionism. While president of the World Zionist Organization, he proved he was a great leader by being able to achieve an
agreement among the other Zionist leaders. He looked at the creation
of a Jewish state, which he summed up in a way that made a lot of
sense to me: "A state cannot be created by decree, but by the forces of
a people and in the course of generations. Even if all the governments
of the world gave us a country, it would only be a gift of words. But if
the Jewish people will go build Palestine, the Jewish State will become a
reality—a fact." That Kfar Hanassi would be named for Weizmann
seemed a fitting tribute, given his British connection and overall
approach.

Habonim was more than a movement that studied the land of Israel. It took action to build up Palestine. We in the movement were
primarily city kids. Our fathers were storeowners and salesmen, small

businessmen, and laborers. What did we know of tilling the soil and milking cows? Very little, and much of what we did know we had read about in books and periodicals. We bought our fruits and vegetables from the fruit and vegetable stand in our neighborhood and our milk from the grocery store. We were only vaguely aware of the origins of these staples. The movement's ultimate goal was to help us work the land when we moved to Palestine, that is, to become *Chalutzim* (pioneers). This was no easy task as we had no practical experience. The idea was to do the preparatory work in Britain and then hit the ground running when we got to the Holy Land. We called this preparation *Hachshara,* and soon enough we would be living it.

A working farm was purchased in the mid-thirties to facilitate *Hachshara*. It would eventually be known as the David Eder Farm, named for Dr. David Eder, a relative of Israel Zangwill and friend of D. H. Lawrence, who, in addition to being a prominent psychoanalyst, had become a major figure in the Zionist movement. Although he had never done any of the work that we would do on the Farm that bore his name, he remained an inspirational figure for many young British Zionists. We simply referred to the David Eder Farm as the Farm, and for many of us it would become our home. I started spending time on the Farm while still a teenager, and tried to spend as much time there as I could. I will never forget the Saturday night trips when I would travel to the Farm. I would help my father close the store at 9:00 P.M. and then hop on my peddle bike and travel the 40 miles to Kent. I remember hearing the church bell toll the midnight hour in the center of Kent, a very loud but dignified chiming that signaled I was very close to the Farm. The church had one of those historic graveyards where famous townspeople had been buried for the last couple of hundred years. While most of the town's citizens were in their beds, those who were still awake could be found in the tavern whose lights were still on. To show you the times, I still remember passing the blacksmith, who I imagined as a large, powerful gent with a hammer and anvil giving a big stallion a new pair of shoes.

While many people my age back in London were busy ending an evening of dancing or other formal socializing, these things never interested me. I had never learned to dance, since the goal of being an English gentleman seemed trivial to me compared to the possibility of becoming a Zionist pioneer. There was nowhere I would rather be on a Saturday night than at the Farm. But while some of the blokes back in London may have gotten to sleep in on Sunday morning, I would be up early in the morning, just as I would during my stint in the army and my years on a kibbutz. And early meant 6 A.M. There would be no leisurely breakfast, just grab a quick bite and get to work.

The Farm was 120 acres, and we rented 80 of them. Although it was a Jewish operation, we had a manager, a local Gentile man who had many years of experience running a farm and whose job was to train us Jewish greenhorns in the art and science of farming. There was a good deal to learn. The farming implements and equipment were largely foreign to us city slickers. Especially when it came to the intricacies of mechanical devices, I was a quick study. Then there was the planting, the plowing, the sowing, the tilling and the harvesting.

During my years on the Farm, we grew and harvested a variety of different crops. There were wheat, potatoes, cabbage, cauliflower, raspberries, and blackberries. Then there were the animals. Naturally, pigs were out of the question. We did have cows to milk and plenty of healthy chickens who were kind enough to lay some eggs that we could sell, as well as a whole lot of sheep, whose wool was our primary interest. But the two animals that I remember best were the strong draught horses used for plowing. Since this was a Jewish operation, they naturally were "Jewish horses," and as strong Zionists only answered to their Hebrew names, which were Shmuel and Devorah. I learned the art of plowing and marveled at the brute force of these two magnificent animals. If you ever worked with Shmuel you would have thought he should have been better named Shimshon (Samson) for the Biblical hero and strongman. But both he and Devorah could also be temperamental and I tried to stay on their good side, rewarding

Leading the bull by the horns or, in this case, by the nose.

their efforts with a well deserved carrot or apple. More than anything, I loved spending time feeding them, grooming them, even cleaning their stables. I became very attached to them, and for a city boy became what one would call a "horse person."

Probably the most dangerous job was looking after the bull. There were some secrets to dealing with animals, and I tried to pick up everything I could from the Farm manager. From ancient times, metal rings of various types have been placed inside a bull's nostrils. When you pull the rings a bit, the bull feels some pain which often makes him more cooperative. I tried not to overuse the rings, and fortunately the bull never seemed to harbor any ill will to me. I may not have been Dr. Doolittle, but I surely loved all the animals on the Farm, even the ornery bull.

While there may have been a great deal of unemployment in much of Britain at the time, there was never any shortage of work to be done on the Farm. It was a harbinger of future life on the kibbutz. And when we wanted to build something, we didn't go looking for a contractor in town; instead we did the work ourselves. When we needed to make concrete for a building we went down to a local quarry to get together the raw materials we needed for our undertaking. We had a one-and-a-half-ton truck and went down to a sand quarry to collect the necessary sand. I drove, and to save money on the petrol I thought we could do this all in one trip, and so the bed of the truck was overflowing with sand. There was only one small problem: getting back to the Farm. There was a steep hill that ran a half mile or so before entering the farm, and with all the sand, the truck would not make it up the hill. Luckily, old Alfy had an idea. I put the truck in reverse and with the low gear was just able to make it back to the Farm.

Just like on the kibbutz, the Farm was not all about work. There was a certain peace and quiet there and when the sun went down, it contrasted sharply with the bright, bustling streets of London. There was no electricity on the Farm, and all we had for light were some kerosene lamps. I loved sitting by my bed reading. My favorite books were historical novels, and it was while reading those books that I could almost feel myself transformed to the place and time I was reading about, whether I was reading *Ivanhoe* or *Rob Roy*, or something similarly exciting. To my grandchildren who were raised with computers and video games, this may sound dull, but I found those nights reading by the light of the kerosene lamps ever so entertaining.

The Farm and the Battle of Cable Street

Part of what made life on the Farm so fulfilling was the rich social life that we enjoyed there. Most of us knew each other through the London Habonim, but there were always new people to meet. Some came from far off, exotic locales such as a very pretty young woman named Naomi, who acquired the well deserved nickname "the Burmese beauty." And if the historical novels gave me a picture of life in faraway places, then meeting people who lived in these places supplemented my curiosity about the world around me. But the vast majority of foreigners who came to the Farm were part of the stream of refugees who were escaping Hitler. Through the efforts of the *Kindertransport*, in which thousands of young people left Germany and other German-controlled countries for a safe haven in England, we met many young people, and the situation that was occurring in Germany was brought even closer to us.

Many friendships were forged during my days on the Farm, and many romances began despite the often grimy and sweaty work we did there. I should say that the Farm was pretty much an egalitarian venture, and the women did the physical labor together with the men. Many marriages can be traced back to the days of the David Eder Farm and if you read a current issue of *Kol Vatikei Habonim*, you can hear the nostalgia of many well into their 70s, 80s and 90s. It was all great fun, but what made it unique was the spirit of the Habonim members. It was on the Farm that the seeds of idealism and drive that would be required on the kibbutz were sown, just like the crops themselves.

We also met *Shlichim*, emissaries who had already taken the plunge and were in the process of building settlements in the Holy Land. In 1938, we met a particularly interesting fellow who, after leaving Austria, had been a founder of the kibbutz at Ein Gav on the eastern end of Lake Kinneret. He was very persuasive, but spoke English with a heavy accent. His name was Teddy Kollek, and he would become the mayor of Jerusalem for some 26 years and was its biggest advocate. And the many Shlichim helped build our resolve that moving to Palestine, with all of its challenges, was not only possible but in fact, necessary. Of course, the events that were occurring in Germany, such as the passage of the Nuremburg Laws, which took away civil rights from the Jews of Germany, and *Kristallnacht,* the dreadful and horrific Night of the Broken Glass, convinced many of us that the Jewish state was the only hope for the long term safety of the Jewish people. And with the militarization of the Rhineland, the outbreak of the Spanish Civil War, the Anschluss of Austria and the Sudeten Crisis, it also looked as if Britain and France were headed for eventual war with Nazism and Fascism, despite the assertions of Prime Minister Chamberlin to the contrary.

THE BATTLE OF CABLE STREET

Before I get too far ahead, I want to mention an important incident that occurred several years before the period on the Farm. Although many Englishmen know about it—and certainly all English Jews who were alive during the 30s or whose parents were do—it is probably not much remembered by later generations. And it bears on what I have written, the rise of Nazism and Fascism. In fact, we had our own troubles in England in the form of homegrown Fascists. They were led by Oswald Mosley, a former Labour MP who had abandoned his initial hero, John Maynard Keynes, and became infatuated with Benito Mussolini during a trip to Italy. He was seeking to bring the same kind of nightmare to England. His group, the Union of British Fascists, often called the Blackshirts because of the uniform that their members wore in imitation of their ideological cousins in Italy, gained something of a following during the mid-30s, no doubt fueled by the economic problems we were experiencing. Mosley would try to stir things up by standing on his ever present soapbox while his Blackshirts looked menacingly around, ready to battle anyone who dared disagree with their rantings or heckled their leader.

Mosley may have overplayed his hand when he decided to organize a large-scale march through the East End on October 4, 1936. This

The Farm and the Battle of Cable Street

The battle of Cable Street: the sign reads "They shall not pass."

was a largely Jewish section and also contained a strong contingent of Irish Catholics and other immigrant groups as well. Though the Board of Jewish Deputies discouraged all Jews from protesting Mosley, many Jews, including me, disregarded the advice of their elders and participated in the brouhaha that was to be known as the Battle of Cable Street.

As I was trying to remember the events of that autumn day nearly 73 years ago, I came upon Bill Fishman's account in the *Guardian* newspaper, who, like myself, was also there. He recounts the events with such clarity as if it had occurred yesterday. Bill, who became a prominent professor, even taped an interview not long ago, and as I listened to it, the events of the day became ever so vivid, ever so powerful. I excerpt a small piece here from his account and I invite the reader back to 1936. Imagine, if you will, this large group of Blackshirts, led by Mosley and under the protection of a large police contingent, some of whom were sympathetic to him, including a contingent on horseback. But we were ready for Mosley, and I stood together with a throng of thousands at the ready. I was one of the younger ones there, but stood with my fellow Jews, union members, communists, and Irish Catholics. Believe it or not, young Alfy had taken a piece of wooden board from an old bus and was ready to make good use of it on the heads or any other piece of anatomy of the invading Blackshirts. Our slogan was *No Pasaran*, they shall not pass, which we had borrowed from the recently fought Battle of Madrid when Republican forces used it as a rallying cry against the Nationalist Forces.

Bill Fishman wrote:

There were masses of marching people. Young people, old people, all shouting 'No Pasaran and one, two, three, four, five-we want Mosley, Dead or Alive.' It was like a mass army gathering, coming from all side streets. Mosley was supposed to arrive at lunchtime but the hours were passing and he hadn't come. Between 3 PM and 3:30 we could see a big army of Blackshirts marching toward the confluence of Commercial Road and Whitechapel Road.

I pushed myself forward and because I was six feet tall I could see Mosley. They were surrounded by an even greater army of police. There was to be this advance of the police force to get the Fascists through. Suddenly, the horses' hooves were flying and the horses were falling down because the young kids were throwing marbles.

I heard this loudspeaker say 'They are going to Cable Street.' Suddenly a barricade was erected there and they put an old lorry (truck) in the middle of the road and old mattresses. The people up the top of the flats, mainly Irish Catholic women, were throwing rubbish on the police. We were all side by side. I was moved to tears to see bearded Jews and Irish Catholic dockers standing up to stop Mosley.

It was indeed an inspirational scene as we stood toe to toe with people so different from ourselves, but most importantly for us Jews, we sent a message loud and clear: Jews cannot be pushed around.

The Farm and the Battle of Cable Street

Mosley's blackshirts were blocked by 300,000 anti-fascists
on the streets of East London.

We will fight not only with the force of our words, but with fists and wooden boards if necessary. When I have discussed events like these with friends over the years they have often expressed surprise that gentle and loveable old Alfy was more than willing to mix it up in a street fight, like some kind of a modern day Daniel Mendoza. It was nothing special really.

Lil was reminding me the other day that sometime in the 1980s we were walking in a park in Evanston with my sister Mimi, when we noticed a group of skinheads, some of whom in addition to their Mohawk hairdos had swastika tattoos emblazoned on their bodies. They had come in a trailer to protest a Zionist meeting that we were attending. Most people would have avoided these folks like the plague. Not my sister Mimi. She went right up to them and informed them that she was Jewish and asked them what they planned to do about it.

Like most bullies when you challenge them, they backed down sure enough. Perhaps it points to something in the Nathan family character. Or maybe something about the Joseph Trumpeldor Chalutz—a spirit that we all were enamored with in our youth. Maybe we were just proud Jews, and in all the years have never tried to hide from the religion of our ancestors. But whatever propelled me to fight in the Battle of Cable Street, it would pale by comparison to what eventually came my way. The Battle of Normandy would come seven and a half years later, but before we get to the fighting on the beaches, I will tell you how Britain and Alfy Nathan ended up across the British Channel and on the shores of France.

PART TWO

The War Years and Beyond

CHAPTER FOUR

The World at War

It is seventy years since the war began. Can you believe it, seventy years? For those who remember the events as they occurred, it does not seem all that long ago. Memories are still vivid. Though there are fewer and fewer veterans of the conflict, there does not appear to be a waning of interest in the events that I experienced. Many movies have been made about the conflict, thousands of books have been written, and the battles and the strategies employed have been gone over and over again. Professors and pundits ask the big questions and go back and forth as they debate the answers. Was the war inevitable? Why did the British and French forces fail so badly during the invasion of France? What accounts for Hitler's obsession with destroying the Jewish people, which sometimes took precedence over his war aims? And perhaps the scariest of all hypothetical questions, could Hitler actually have won? And I have my own questions, questions that have been on my mind since I was a sixteen year-old, and these events began unfolding. For instance, why did Hitler not invade Britain? I have long had my doubts whether we could have successfully resisted Hitler's armies, but, thank goodness, we were never put to the test of an outright invasion. But before we get to the Battle of Britain, I will share with you the origins of the conflict.

It was a war that was not supposed to happen. Mr. Chamberlain, our prime minister, after signing an agreement with Hitler in 1938, held up that magic piece of paper and promised us that at long last we had achieved "Peace for our time." It sounded too good to be true, and it was. Scarcely less than one year later, war came to Europe when Germany invaded Poland on September 1, 1939. Since we had signed a treaty with Poland, England and France were now officially at war with Germany. It is true that little transpired other than the signing of the Hitler-Stalin Pact, which divided that poor country between the two rival dictators. We did not intervene to help Poland, but instead sent troops to France to prepare for a possible invasion in the West. That was a period we call the "Phony War." But what was to come was very real indeed. The man sounding the alarm bells for several years as Germany grew stronger was none other than Winston Churchill. I had always liked Churchill, admired him a good deal and believed him to be a friend of the Zionist cause and the Jewish people. This I believed, despite the presence of the terrible White Paper, begun under Mr. Chamberlain, which limited Jewish immigration to Palestine at precisely the time it was so desperately needed.

In the world according to Alfy, it was Mr. Churchill, who by dint of word and deed saved our country from impending disaster. To show you what I mean, I excerpted parts of two of his speeches here, not because I want to share with you the greatness of his words, and let me tell you, he was even better than Obama at speechmaking if my younger readers can believe that, but because it will give you a sense of just how dire the times we lived in were. Mr. Churchill assumed office in the middle of the battles raging in France, and the battles were not going well. But you will see how he managed to rally a tired and weary and, dare I say, frightened people on May 13, 1940, shortly after assuming office, with these words:

> *I say to the House as I say to those who have joined this government, I have nothing to offer but blood, toil, tears and sweat. We have before us an ordeal of the most grievous kind. We have before us many, many months of struggle and of suffering. You ask what is*

our policy? I say it is to wage war by land, sea and air. War with all our might and with all the strength God has given us, and to wage war against a monstrous tyranny never surpassed in the dark and lamentable catalogue of human crime. That is our policy. You ask, what is our aim? I can answer in one word: It is victory, victory at all costs, victory in spite of all terror, victory, however long and hard the road may be; for without victory, there is no survival. Let that be realized; no survival for the British Empire, no survival for all that the British Empire has stood for, no survival for the urge and impulse of the ages, that mankind will move forward toward its goal. But I take up my task with buoyancy and hope. I feel sure that our cause will not be suffered to fail among men. At this time I feel entitled to claim the aid of all, and I say, 'Come then, let us go forward together with our united strength.'

Winston Churchill, Prime Minister of the United Kingdom from 1940 to 1945 and from 1951 to 1955

Wikimedia Commons

Our armies were well on their way to total collapse. British and French troops were surrounded in the area near Dunkirk in the last week of May, and a massive rescue operation ensued in an effort to bring them to Britain. Over 300,000 British and French troops made it to safety, though it was a harrowing journey. I remember seeing throngs of troops at various railway stations in England during this period. True, they made it to safety, but when you looked in their eyes you could see the remnants of the terror that is war itself. Perhaps, more than anyone, those men knew what we were all in for. Their downtrodden and ashen faces represented the blow that the free world had taken since the war had begun, and now Germany seemed invincible.

The situation in France was very dire. The Germans were at the gates of Paris and the French would eventually surrender, and worse yet, some would openly collaborate with the Nazis with the formation of the Vichy government. Their crimes would include handing over Jews to the Gestapo and other such horrendous acts of betrayal and cowardice. And the stark reality pointed to Britain being the next candidate for invasion by the Third Reich. Churchill was under tremendous pressure by many, both from within the government and outside it, to enter into a treaty with Hitler. This way, people reasoned, at least we would be able keep our empire or a portion of it. And from the looks of it, our country did not look strong enough to withstand an invasion. By now, everyone knew the word "blitzkrieg." And although the Luftwaffe would pound our cities, which we will speak about soon enough, we would survive. If there was any question of making peace with Hitler, Mr. Churchill crushed that when he delivered the inspirational speech known as "Their finest hour" on June 18, several days before the French capitulated. He set the stakes for what was about to occur, and it is obvious that the stakes were high. Much was expected from every man, woman, and child in Britain.

What General Weygard has called the Battle of France is over. I expect that the Battle of Britain is about to begin. Upon this battle depends the survival of Christian civilization. Upon it depends our own British life, and the long continuity of our institutions and our Empire. The whole fury and might of the enemy must very soon be turned on us. Hitler knows that he will have to break us in this island or lose the war. If we can stand up to him, all Europe may be freed and the life of the world may move forward into broad, sunlit uplands. But if we fail, then the whole world, including the United States, including all that we have known and cared for will sink into the abyss of a new Dark Age made more sinister and

British troops escaping from Dunkirk in lifeboats, 1940

perhaps more protracted by the lights of perverted science. Let us therefore brace ourselves to our duties, and so bear ourselves, that if the British Empire and its Commonwealth last for a thousand years, then we will still say, "This was their finest hour."

The bombings, or as Mr. Churchill called it, the Battle of Britain, began in earnest in August 1940. I had been living on the Farm on a full-time basis and made my primary contribution to the war effort through the production of food, which was critical at that point. There was severe rationing at that time, and although there would also be similar rationing of many goods such as meat in the United States, it was nowhere as extreme as in Britain during the war. What made the situation so critical was that the Nazis were determined to starve the British Isles, and with the deadly U-boat campaign underway, it was very difficult for supplies to reach England from America. Therefore, whatever could be produced domestically was critical, and all priority was given to feeding the armed forces. As Napoleon stated, "An army marches on its stomach." The British people proved to have a remarkable capacity for sacrifice, and of course our propaganda very much enforced the notion that we were all in this together, and that the nation's needs should always be put ahead of the individual's. There were signs at major transportation centers which contained the stark words, "Is this trip really necessary?" After all, no one wanted to be seen as selfish and hurting the cause of a nation at war.

Speaking of food, an interesting development occurred in the Zionist movement in Britain at this time. A prominent Baltic Jew, I think he was from Latvia, had been training Jewish youngsters in the fishing trade in the hopes that they would be able to use their skills and become fishermen, not on the Baltic Sea, but on the Mediterranean, the Jordan River, and the Sea of Galilee. He managed to escape together with his fleet to England shortly before the war, and was anxious to train the British Zionist youth to become commercial fishermen just as he had been doing earlier. His plan was approved by the Zionist Federation and volunteers were sought from the Farm, among other places. Yours truly was quick to volunteer and anxious to learn all there was to learn about fishing. It was typical of me in the sense that learning new things, practical things, always excited me. Unfortunately, the plan was soon cancelled. The Nazis had begun to attack British fishing boats in their effort to starve us, and the Zionist Federation was worried about a potential tragedy if Jewish youngsters were killed at sea. So my fishing career was over before it had begun.

The Nathan family took many interesting turns during the war. My father did his part despite already being middle-aged. He was helping with air raid precautions, warning people of impending German air raids. He often had the chance to see the effects of what happened when people were unable to flee in time, certainly glad that his younger children were not still in London. The Germans targeted the large industrial cities for the majority of their bombings, and most of the youngsters were evacuated to the countryside. People gathered in the underground tube stations, what Americans call subway stations, to avoid the terrible bombs. Sometimes they slept there through the night. Families had their own spots and in the darkness and dampness of those stations, people did their best to keep a collective stiff upper lip.

Barry and Mimi were both evacuated. Initially, they spent a short time in Reading during the Phony War, and later returned to London when the danger subsided. Eventually they were sent to Cornwall, a relatively sleepy area in the far southwest of the country. Mimi and Barry rode on the train together, and Barry, who was still just a young boy, was understandably upset about being taken away from family and protested as many children surely did. He was going to get off the train before it got underway and after hearing of his plans, one of the teachers grabbed him by the scruff of the neck and apparently he calmed down. Mimi did her best to keep track of Barry once they arrived in Cornwall, but with a throng of people exiting the train, she had lost track of him. She went to look for him the next day, but couldn't find him anywhere. She went to the mayor of the village, and they went all over looking for him and finally located him in a village three miles away staying at the home of the local pharmacist. What happened? The pharmacist's wife had gone to the train station to pick up the young boy who was supposed to be staying with them, but for some reason this boy was not on the train. Her own sons were very much looking forward to having a new lad to pal around with, and were noticeably disappointed when the boy was not there. Instead, they saw Barry standing there, waiting for his family to pick him up, and told him to hop in the motorcar. It was very irresponsible of them, but eventually everything was straightened out.

Things were very tough economically. Barry was back with a family in the village but they apparently were very poor. Mimi would check on him as often as she could and would bring him various things that my father had sent her. Once she brought him a pair of sandals. Then, upon seeing him again, she noticed that he was not wearing them. She

The bombing of London

asked him why and though he tried to dismiss it she insisted on an answer and discovered that the family had actually sold the sandals. So these were very tough times. Fortunately, the young are resilient and what adults view with disfavor as inconvenience or worse, the young sometimes see as a sort of natural adventure. After several years Mimi and Barry were able to join the rest of the family in Balham where Kit, Sally and their families were able to get a flat in a time in which available housing was scarce.

Balham had become famous for a particularly tragic incident. People, like my siblings, and others in the major cities would take refuge and huddle in the middle of the night in underground train stations during the Blitz. In Balham, the tube station was filled with civilians during one particularly bad night of bombing on October 14th 1940. Though this was the safest place one could have been during a raid, the German bomb was a direct hit on the station, causing water and gas lines to burst and ultimately 64 people were killed. With the ascendency of the RAF and the war turning in our direction, things had changed but Hitler had new weapons that he developed for us. V-1 and V-2 rockets landed throughout England in 1944 and had we not captured and secured the launch sites on the coast of France and Holland, these would have continued with more people dying. Fortunately, in our family it was only property that was destroyed. Clothes were shredded but not limbs. No one in our clan was hurt or killed but 10,000 civilians cannot say the same, for that is the number killed in these attacks and many more were wounded. This was in addition to the 43,000 innocent souls that lost their lives during the London Blitz several years earlier.

As feeding the military was the major priority, rations were paltry for civilians. People were allowed 1 ½ eggs per week, 2 ounces of butter or margarine, and 2 ounces of cheese and very limited amounts of meat or chicken. Of course, our American allies rallied behind us and this included members of our extended family. Kit remembers to this day the care packages that would arrive from our Aunt Sonya (Sarah) in New York complete with Hershey bars and raisins. These items must have tasted like the finest Russian caviar when one is living on relatively meager rations. With the problems inherent in corresponding during the war and with the family getting the flat in Balham, our American relatives did not have the new address. Aunt Sonya was not to be deterred. The Yiddish newspaper, the *Jewish Daily Forward* in New York assisted with locating relatives across the ocean during the war, and with help of the British Red Cross she was able to contact the family.

My sisters had met our first American relatives in 1938 in the person of our first cousin Herman Lubens, son of my aunt Pauline, my father's sister. It is an interesting tale because Herman was not admitted to medical school in the early thirties due to the infamous Jewish quotas in the United States that limited Jewish enrollment in universities and professional schools. What makes it all quite ironic is that Herman was able to secure admission to medical school in Germany as the

Nazis were taking over. He remained there throughout much of the thirties, and apparently there were other American Jews who attended medical school in Germany at the time. Though he suffered no persecution nor was forced to leave, he must have been terribly disheartening to witness what the Nazis were doing to his fellow Jews. On a trip through Europe with his father before returning to the United States, Herman came to London and visited with my sisters and other family members. During the war, Herman's brother Milton was stationed in England along with many other American servicemen and was very nice to my siblings, taking them to USO functions and the like, which they greatly enjoyed. He provided access to luxuries like Coca Cola and donuts that were in short supply. His kindness, like those directed by many American servicemen to our people, was greatly appreciated, but in the case of Milton, it was made all the more special since he was our cousin. We were all in this war together.

Many of the men in the family would serve in the military. Kit's husband, Dave Solomon, joined a reconnaissance unit, and after serving in the Middle East, was heavily involved in the Italian campaigns, landing on the Anzio beachhead and participating in some of the bloodiest fighting of the war. Unlike my own unit, which you will hear about shortly, he joined an outfit which had a lot of Jewish fellows from the East End and they suffered a very high casualty rate. From Anzio, he moved to participate in the liberation of Rome. Dave and Kit would visit the beachheads at Anzio years later, paying tribute at the graves of the many brave men who died on that Italian beach. Dave was stationed in Germany at the end of the war and since he spoke Yiddish well was a participant in the interrogations of German officers. He told me that every one of the bunch would claim, "I was not a Nazi" which obviously was not always true.

My brother Sid was inducted in 1940, and rose in the ranks of the non-commissioned officers, ultimately becoming a sergeant. He served in an artillery unit and with his strong but dignified manner was very well respected by the men in his company. His unit took the same path through Europe that mine did, and we eventually met up square in the middle of all the fighting in Holland. Before I start on that story, I will tell you of the events that led to my induction in His Majesty's Armed Forces.

When I turned eighteen in 1941, I went to the local induction office, but they did not induct me. Apparently, my work on the Farm was considered important enough that I was given an agricultural deferment. (Again this gets back to the central role that food production played in the war effort.) Then, by 1943, the government decided it was going to draft people who were working in the agricultural sector. At the time I had two very close friends, Ronnie Shneerson and Alec Marmot, who were together with me on the Farm and in the same situation. The three of us decided to join the RAF in the hope of becoming pilots. Why pilots, you ask? The prestige of the RAF had never been higher. Many people are familiar with the famous statement of Mr. Churchill's, "Never in the field of human conflict was so much owed by so many to so few." He was referring, of course, to the RAF's repelling of the Luftwaffe in the skies over Britain, and sure enough, that was a turning point in the war.

Well, we went down to the office and were put through a battery of tests. Ronnie and Alec were both accepted, but I was rejected. It was for the reason that disqualified many an aspiring pilot; inadequate vision. In my case I had one bad eye, which was obviously an impediment to becoming a successful pilot. I did not take the news very well. In fact, I took it rather poorly. I was tremendously disappointed at the turn of events. I could already see myself in my flight suit, complete with RAF wings and engaged in a dogfight with one of the Luftwaffe's top aces, or something of the sort. Now my dreams were dashed with the simple mark of an optometrist's pen. As for my two friends, they both successfully completed their training and entered the Royal Air Force. What happened to them? Ronnie was killed in action in a mission over Germany and Alec survived the war and was to join me later as a member of Kfar Hanassi.

The draft board allowed me to return to the Farm, but told me not to get too comfortable in my civilian surroundings as I would be called up soon enough. And when that day came, they asked me as part of the routine screening process if my parents were naturalized British citizens. I told them that I knew that they were born in Russia, but was unsure whether they had been naturalized. They told me to find out, but I explained to them that my family had been evacuated and I had not been able to find out where they were. The board strongly suggested that I find them and get the answer to the naturalization question. On subsequent occasions when I was called before the board, I told them that I had still been unable to find them. They eventually tired of my constant excuses and must have decided that they would provide me with a little bit of incentive. So one day an envelope arrived in the mail from the Soviet Embassy in London. In it was a tersely written letter on official stationery which essentially stated that it had come to their attention that my parents were born in Russia and therefore I was to be considered a Soviet citizen. As such, I was obligated to serve in the Red Army and was to report to the Soviet Embassy for immediate induction. It did not take too many newsreels from the Battle of Stalingrad to make me realize that this was a bad deal indeed, so I went to the induction center as fast as my feet would take me, and making no reference to the letter, informed the officials that I had indeed located my family and was pleased to report that my parents were naturalized citizens.

Like all new recruits, the first stop on my odyssey consisted of six weeks of basic training. In my case, that training took place in the city of Leicester. Since there was an acute shortage of housing available on the base, many of us bunked in the horse stables. Fortunately, from my experiences on the Farm, I had grown accustomed to the smell of stables and I adjusted well to the Spartan life that was basic training. Upon completion, it was now a question of what military occupation and to what unit to assign Private Nathan. It was decided that due to my mechanical background and my work on the Farm, I would be assigned to the Royal Engineers.

"What, pray tell, would I be doing in the Royal Engineers?" I asked the officer in charge. The captain, a tall, athletic-looking chap with a spine so straight it looked as if it was going to snap, cleared his throat and told me, "You will be operating a steamroller," and in my typical, off-the-cuff manner, I quipped, "Gee, that's not going to get me to Berlin very fast." To which he responded, "You want to get to Berlin fast, do you, Private Nathan?" And again not being able to resist the temptation to respond affirmatively, came back with, "Sure, let's take Berlin and get this damn war over with, sir." If the first rule of thumb in the military is never to volunteer for anything, I had violated it, or as some say, never wish for anything, you just might get it. And the officer at this point realized he had a live one. He wrote something in the folder marked "Nathan, A." with some official looking numbers and letters next to them, and told me that I was being assigned to the Tank Corps, in my case, an amphibious armour unit. The officer then managed a smile and wished me luck, which I guess he realized I was going to need. Of course, I did not know anything about tanks or amphibious armour, but was soon to find out that it was going to figure heavily in the planning for Operation Overlord, the invasion of Europe, which was already well into the planning stages. I was indeed on the fast track to Berlin. (I should add that of course the Russians, in some of the bloodiest fighting in the war, would take Berlin, although surely we and our American allies could have gotten there first, but alas that is the subject for another day.)

Armoured training took place in an area called Ashton-under-Lyme, a small town about seven miles east of Manchester. There are large tracts of moorland in the greater Manchester area, and despite being so close to an industrial area, it is actually quite beautiful. One of the benefits of being in Manchester was that it allowed me to spend as much time as possible with the local Habonim people, though many were in the service just like me. I found Manchester to my liking, for in addition to the Jewish community that I developed ties with; the working class townspeople that resided there seemed especially friendly.

Wikimedia Commons

Sherman DD (Duplex Drive) amphibious tank

After armoured training, I was assigned to the 13/18th Royal Hussars Battalion, 27th Armoured Brigade. Both the 13th and the 18th had storied histories as cavalry regiments and had been consolidated in 1922. During the early years of the war, this unit had been attached to the 9th Armoured Division and later to the 79th. Everything changed in October 1943, when it was decided that the brigade should be attached to the 3rd Infantry Division in preparation for the invasion of France. Again, the 3rd Division had a storied tradition, having distinguished themselves in the Crimean and Boer Wars as well as World War One. It had been part of the British Expeditionary Force that had been evacuated from Dunkirk, and as you can imagine, there were veterans of the unit who had waited quite a while to redeem themselves and the reputation of the Division. They would now get their chance.

The 27th was critical to the success of what would presumably be a beachhead landing. We were equipped with 250 amphibious tanks. They were called DD tanks (the abbreviation stood for Duplex Drive, although we would often jokingly call them Donald Duck). In fact, they were modified Shermans that were specifically developed for the landings and D-Day. I found out much later that the technology was the brainchild of a Hungarian-born engineer working in Britain named Nicholas Straussler. Straussler's big contribution was the development of a floatation screen, a screen that folded up and consisted of waterproof canvas. For this reason they were called "swimming tanks," which is precisely what they did when used correctly, which in the 27th armoured division became job number one. I should also say that it was General Percy Hobart, a great innovator, who pushed the idea to the powers in Whitehall that the thing could really work and would not be a military disaster, Of course, the great benefit of being able to land tanks directly on the beaches is that it provides immediate support for the infantry troops.

The ironic thing about the amphibious tanks is that while they had not been used very much in actual combat, it was the Germans who had in fact experimented a lot with them, hoping to use them in the invasion of England. Now the tables would be turned. We trained for the invasion in the Hebrides on the Scottish coast. These are a series of islands that were ideal for this purpose. There is an old military saying, "The more sweat on the training field, the less blood on the battlefield." We would simulate the invasion time after time by attacking the Scottish coast, where we met with surprisingly little resistance. One of the most challenging aspects in all of this was waterproofing the tanks. The key element was to carefully apply foam over the engine of the tank. Mistakes were frequently made, and that meant that the tank would not move through the water. You would be stuck there, sitting on the turret, helplessly waiting to be picked up by one of the naval vessels that had been assigned to the exercise. Our commanders would let us sit good and long out there until our clothing began getting very wet and we felt uncomfortable and began shivering. The lesson began to sink in because a similar mistake during the invasion would have far dire consequences.

Relaxing at the Farm while on leave during training in the army.

We finally got the word that we were leaving the Scottish coast, and eventually travelled down to Portsmouth, where we would await our orders. As we entered the south of England, I was struck by the fact that the entire part of the country had been cut off from the rest of England. In the period immediately preceding the invasion, no non-military personnel were allowed in or out. The concern was security of course, and even though everyone, including the Germans, knew that the invasion was imminent, the idea was to try to limit those who knew both the time and place it would occur.

CHAPTER FIVE

Landing at Normandy

Portsmouth was simply overflowing with troops, all nervously anticipating the order for invasion. Men would play cards, write a letter to a sweetheart, or simply try to grab some sleep. The main problem keeping us in England was the inclement weather. But we did not know that on the morning of June 5, meteorologists were predicting a break in the storms that we had been experiencing. General Eisenhower, the Supreme Allied Commander, issued the following as the General Order of the Day for June 6:

> *Soldiers, Sailors, and Airmen of the Allied Expeditionary Force!*
> *You are about to embark upon the Great Crusade, toward which*
> *we have striven these many months. The eyes of the world are upon*
> *you. The hope and prayers of liberty-loving people everywhere march*
> *with you. In company with our brave Allies and brothers-in-arms*
> *on other Fronts, you will bring about the destruction of the*
> *German war machine, the elimination of Nazi tyranny over the*
> *oppressed peoples of Europe, and security for ourselves in a*
> *free world.*
>
> *Your task will not be an easy one. Your enemy is well trained,*
> *well equipped and battle-hardened. He will fight savagely.*

But this is the year 1944! Much has happened since the Nazi triumphs of 1940-41. The United Nations have inflicted upon the Germans great defeats, in open battle, man-to-man. Our air offensive has seriously reduced their strength in the air and their capacity to wage war on the ground. Our Home Fronts have given us an overwhelming superiority in weapons and munitions of war, and placed at our disposal great reserves of trained fighting men. The tide has turned! The free men of the world are marching together to Victory!

I have full confidence in your courage, devotion to duty and skill in battle. We will accept nothing less than full Victory!

Good luck! And let us beseech the blessing of Almighty God upon this great and noble undertaking.

Since it was still June 5, we did not yet know about the General Order, and we were still resting when we got the word to assemble. As the entire brigade was standing at attention, several jeeps pulled up, and it was plain that there was some big brass present. And the brass could not have been bigger when the two men emerged from the jeep. They turned out to be none other than General Eisenhower and Field Marshall Montgomery, the man who had defeated Rommel at El Alamein scarcely a year and a half earlier, ensuring that the Nazis would not make it to Palestine. (This victory in the Battle of Egypt in 1942 was also important in that it was our first major victory over Germany. It was Mr. Churchill who said in his speech after the victory, "Now this is not the end. This is not even the beginning of the end. But it is, perhaps, the end of the beginning.")

The two great generals had come to tell us something we probably long suspected, that of the many men assembled along the coast of England for the invasion, we would be the first to land, the spearhead of the spearhead, so to speak. General Eisenhower, the man who would one day become president of the United States, along with our commander, General Montgomery, had one sentence for us before they would rush off, presumably to express similar sentiments to other units. "Gentlemen, you have the honor of leading the democratic forces into Europe." Well, if anyone expected a bunch of cheering and giving it the old hip, hip hooray for the cause, they were sadly disappointed. That's not what many of us shouted, but what we did shout was loud enough to draw some angry looks from our officers. Our response was so uniform it must have sounded rehearsed. We blurted out, "Go to bloody Hell!"

Was it a bit disrespectful? I suppose so, but what were they going to do, court martial the whole lot of us? They needed us on that beach. And the tough thing of it was you knew what was waiting for you on that beach. A lot of machine gun nests pointing their weapons right at you, anti-tank ditches, mortars, and a lot of other lethal stuff straight from the pages of the Wehrmacht Welcome Wagon. As important as our job was, it was hard to be too enthusiastic about doing it. No pep talk could hide the reality of the mission. Getting on the beach was going to be tough as all hell. And once we were on the beach that was what it would resemble, hell. But we had to do it. And to take nothing away from Generals Montgomery and Eisenhower, for they were great men, great soldiers, and great leaders, it was up to us young grunts to do the fighting and unfortunately, the dying. They would get the credit or the blame for the invasion, but it would be our lives on the line. So I suppose we had earned the right to say, "Go to bloody hell."

D-Day, Operation Neptune, or Normandy—take your pick. The weather had been stormy for a good number of days and the invasion had been cancelled several times. But once we got the go ahead, this time on the 5th of June, to go the following morning, we knew it was on for real. We got into the landing crafts, which took some time. As a matter of fact, once we got aboard, we waited for several hours off the coast of Portsmouth until all our equipment was loaded, just floating in the water. As you looked around, you could see there were massive numbers of ships filled with men and their instruments of war for miles around. It seemed as if there were more men in the water that day than there were fish. It was a flotilla unlike any other that these eyes or any other pair of eyes have seen or are likely to see again. While we were waiting, the enormity of it all finally hit me. I was going into combat. I was going to have to kill the enemy. And all of a sudden I began to cry to myself. What was I crying about? "How can I, loveable old Alfy Nathan, the peaceful and ethical person that I thought I was, take the life of another human being?" But once you hit that shore and the shells were flying all around, you were forced to react. Very few people froze up or panicked because all of your training takes over, and perhaps even more importantly, your adrenaline kicks in and somehow you move forward. And being young and strong, you don't think you are going to die, although it never hurts to pray a bit.

Many have asked me over the years, "Alfy, what was it really like on the beaches of Normandy?" They have seen some of the movies made about the landings, films like "The Longest Day" and "Saving Private Ryan," and everyone is curious to know how much was real and how much was Hollywood? Well, I saw "Saving Private Ryan" when it first hit the theaters and it always struck me as being as authentic as any movie could possibly be. It portrays well the chaos of those initial moments of the invasion, but the only way to really know what it was like to be on the beach that day was to actually have been there in person.

Fortunately, we survived in greater numbers than the planners and our commanders expected us to. We later found out that there was a unit that was supposed to disembark after the initial invasion (when most of the men would land with the beaches being secured) with the same unit markings, the same tanks, the same spare parts as our own. Why? They did not expect most of us to make it, but, thank God, most of us were fortunate. I was almost not one of the lucky ones. There we were, in about three feet of shallow water, and the front of the landing craft was getting ready to open. (I will never forget that our crafts were all made in New Orleans, that historic and fun-loving city famous for jazz and Mardi Gras, but I will forever associate it with

Landing at Normandy

The British 2nd Army at SWORD Area: (above left) Infantry waiting to move off "Queen White" Beach while under enemy fire; (right) Commandos of the First Special Service Brigade landing from an LCI(S) on "Queen Red" Beach at la Breche.

Normandy.) Our lieutenant turned to me and said, "O.K., Nathan, lead the way," but I deferred to his rank. I said, "Sir, with all due respect, you should be the one to lead us." Whether I embarrassed him into going out first, he took my words to heart and proceeded to leave the craft. It was the last thing he ever did, because we had pulled up right over a bomb crater. The landing craft pulled away and positioned itself in a different location and feeling that it was safe to get out, the tanks and trucks of the unit began to roll off. But now we had to proceed ashore without an officer, which of course would not be unique on the beaches of Normandy during that bloody day.

I do not like to harp too much on what went on during the morning of June the 6th, except to say that the fighting on the beach was just plain tough. There was shelling all over the place. Men all around me were being shot up, some killed, some badly wounded. You just can't think about it, you just have to move. The mission was to get on the beach and take it. Despite the difficulties, it was clear the Germans could not stop us. The whole idea of our landing on Sword Beach, the easternmost of the five beaches that composed the Normandy landings, was so that we could directly attack the city of Caen, which is the nearest city to the beach. Some thought we could take the entire city by the end of the day, since we were able to pierce what was called the Atlantic Wall, the defensive measures put in by the Germans to keep us from getting off the beach. And while we were doing well and had entered the city, we had to withdraw because the infantry, which was still trying to get on the beach, could not keep up with us.

General Montgomery thought that the fighting around the city of Caen would last for a few days at most. He was wrong. It was an extremely difficult battle and would take nearly five weeks to liberate all of Caen. This should counter a common misconception about Normandy. Most people think that just because the landings were successful that we immediately got on the road to Germany, something like planning a cross country trip with the Motor Club. That was not the case. We faced great obstacles every step of the way. A panzer unit relentlessly counterattacked and was a big problem; the German resistance was fanatical, and their fighting was professional. Fortunately, General Montgomery's idea was to break the back of the German army by pounding their positions with constant bombings, softening them so that the armour and infantry would have an easier time—and on this point Monty sometimes disagreed with his American colleagues. I believe they called this tactic "dazing," and he used it heavily during the Battle of Caen.

The bombing and shelling lasted throughout the ensuing battle. At night I needed to get some shuteye, so I dug a hole and put the truck over the hole, and then hooked up a few wires from the truck to give me some light to read in the hole. I figured as long as it was not a direct hit, I would be fine, and in between reading my book, I managed to grab some sleep until our attack commenced the next day.

In the middle of Caen there was a magnificent church with a tall steeple. The Germans had positioned themselves in the steeple and

Moving through Caen

The ruins of Caen-July 1944

were doing tremendous damage, inflicting significant casualties on us. You could not even go to the toilet in peace because the Germans would just pick you off before you finished doing your business. Once, several of us were moving about, when the sergeant yelled "down." And my face found the earth in a millisecond. Yet, when I looked up, I noticed that the man to one side of me was dead, the other was shot in the stomach. You learned a valuable lesson: when you get an order, you'd better react and react fast. It has to be automatic, as if you were a machine and not a man. Because if you didn't, you would be history.

Rifle fire, machine gun fire everywhere, but the Germans were not moving out of that church. We asked our allies, the good old Americans, for some aerial assistance in dislodging them, and sure enough, huge bombers soon filled the French sky, dropping their massive payload on the area. The noise was deafening. We were cheering wildly, and if there had been any residual British anger over the loss of our American colonies a century and half earlier, it was gone as we waited for the Yank bombers to finish their mission. Guess what? When the dust and the debris settled, the church was reduced to nothing but rubble, but the steeple still stood in the midst of the destruction, and the Germans were still there and firing away at us. Eventually we took them out.

Much of Caen was destroyed in the weeks of fighting. It was as if a giant earthquake had come and uprooted so many old buildings. Fortunately, some civilians managed to escape as our boys in the RAF had dropped leaflets informing them of our plans to take the city. Still, several hundred civilians died, but that is the terrible cost of war. They call it "collateral damage," but that is just a way of saying that war is so terribly inhuman and unfair. Of course, when you saw the look of the French people, the old women with tears in their eyes and the young children who smiled at you after enduring four years of occupation, you knew what was at stake. You began to understand the meaning of the word "liberation," even though it came at such a steep price.

Our ultimate goal was, of course, Germany itself. The path our army was to take to advance through France was a northern route, alongside the North Sea, into Belgium, Holland, and across the Rhine and into Germany. Traveling through the Low Countries presented many unique challenges. Until we reached Antwerp, we did not have access to a port, and with our swift advance, we were faced with the problem of every modern army since Napoleon; we were having difficulty maintaining our supply lines. We turned to our American allies again for help, and as usual, the Yanks came through. They sent a transportation unit, trucks filled with food and other supplies. These were not the typical army trucks but were semi-trailers. None of us had ever seen such big rigs before. What was an even bigger surprise were the men that drove those large vehicles. They were an all-black unit, and the only whites in the unit were the officers. Most of us had very little contact with black people before, as England had very few blacks at the time. But I will tell you one thing. Those fellows sure were glad to see us. They worked with us for a time, and I could tell that they were not used to being treated like equals. They were a fine group, and I learned a good deal about America speaking with these fellows, though what I learned about how Black people were treated certainly troubled me.

In Holland we ran into some problems. The Germans were desperate to slow our advance, and they figured if they could flood the area, we would not be able to move our troops and equipment through. Holland is a country largely reclaimed from the sea, so although flooding sounds like a terrible thing to do, they did it. But they did not stop us as we were very good at finding areas that were at least partially dry to get through. By October we were in Belgium and approaching Antwerp. The Germans were particularly stubborn in Antwerp. The port was of enormous strategic value, and if you remember the Battle of the Bulge, the German winter offensive, one of its aims was to retake that beautiful city. The Germans were all over the islands surrounding Antwerp, and we had one heck of a hard time dislodging them. We were fighting in water that was sometimes up to our chest. We were successful, but it was bloody.

I never knew how many men I killed because it was not like hand-to-hand fighting. You just knew they were firing at you and you were firing at them, and when they stopped firing, they were dead, wounded, or had retreated. But the knowledge of what you did, however necessary, does haunt you. You have to live with it. The sergeant said to us at the beginning of our training with great conviction, "You got to learn to kill," and when I first heard it I did not think I could ever learn to do that. But you learn soon enough that it is either them or you. It was General Patton who once said, "The object of war is not to die for your country. It's to make the other poor bastard die for his," and I suppose that is the sad truth of the matter.

I drove a truck once we reached France, and had the idea that I would like to have a Magen David in the front of the truck. I knew that this was not standard operating procedure, but it was important to me. I suppose some would think that I might have been interested in the heavenly protection that such a powerful symbol might have afforded

With the Star of David flag. Looking fit and a bit menacing.

me. But that was not my primary motivation. For one thing, I realized that the invasion of Europe was not only about the British, the French, or the Dutch people. It was not only about defeating Hitler, it was also about saving Jewish lives. Not that we knew the complete story of the Holocaust, but we knew it was very bad, and the sooner we got to Germany the more likely we would be able to save Jewish lives. To the Jewish soldier not only in the British army, but among all the Allies, the mission to liberate Europe had special significance. But my main objective in having the small flag there was to meet and make contact with other Jews, both those like me who were in uniform and civilians we happened to meet as we made our way to Germany.

I approached the battalion commander, a lieutenant colonel, and after considering the matter, he gave me the O.K. to proceed. But then I ran into problems. The company commander, a major, came to me and told me this was not a Jewish unit and to get my Star of David off of his truck. I told him that our battalion commander had already given me permission, and if he had a problem he should take it up with the colonel. The major was more than a touch unhappy about my response, but what could he do? He was bound by the chain of command. The major was from a well off family and had attended either Oxford or Cambridge, and liked to remind people of his upper class status. Like many from his class, he tended to look down on others less privileged, which happened to include the vast majority of British society. Whether he was an out and out anti-Semite is debatable, but to me he was certainly anti-Alfy, which at the time amounted to the same thing. Though I do not regret at all that Magen David, in fact, I am very proud of what I did

The platoon's senior enlisted man was a sergeant major with one of the heaviest cockney accents I ever heard, and I have heard a good deal of them. He was straight from the London docks, and before he joined the army many years earlier, he had indeed worked as a longshoreman. That I have conveniently forgotten his name does not mean I have forgotten the rough looking scowl he wore as his trademark. His feelings about Jewish people were unlike the major's more reserved style; it was very much out in the open.

As the only Jew in the unit, I was always on guard, but though I had a problem with the sergeant major and the major, the vast majority of the men in the unit were fine fellows indeed. We all worked well together, and I did not sense any anti-Semitism from them. The unit had very good fighting spirit, and I was proud to serve with these fellows. I should say that in looking back on things, the Star of David did indeed bring me good luck. Otherwise I would not be writing these words today.

As tough as the war was, humor managed to make an occasional appearance. We captured a good many Germans. As the fighting lagged on and as our victory became inevitable to most in the Wehrmacht, there were large groups of German soldiers who began to surrender at will. Once our unit caught a mid level German officer, a major, I think.

As one of our interrogators left him and walked by several of us, he began to laugh. That was highly unusual, so we all wanted to know what was so funny. Apparently, the German officer knew some English and when given a cigarette, spoke to the interrogator about the endless aerial assaults from both sides, "Ven you British bomb, ve duck, ven ve Germans bomb, you duck, but ven ze Americans bomb, ve all duck."

In Holland I saw some fellows pass by and noticed that they were wearing the same unit emblem as my brother Sid. I was flabbergasted. We had not seen each other in a long time, and though I knew which unit he was in, since he had been there for nearly four years, he did not know much about where I was serving or that we had virtually been traveling along the same route to Germany, essentially fighting as part of the same campaign. I saw a man with enough stripes on him to know what was going on, and asked him if he was acquainted with a Sgt. Nathan. Indeed he was, and as soon as I got some liberty, I went to Sid's command headquarters and was told to wait for him. A few hours later, my older brother arrived. You should have seen the look on his face. Complete and utter amazement! Talk about a small world! I would like to tell the reader that our long awaited reunion was tearful and deeply emotional, but you have to understand the time and the place. There were men all around, and we were in the middle of a war against a brutal enemy. And we were British to boot. So we did not show too much emotion, although our hearts certainly felt a connection beyond what our mouths were able to express. It was wonderful seeing him. There are really not words adequate enough to explain how I really felt that day in Holland. From taking our Hebrew lessons with Rabbi Lipshutz in the East End to eating fish and chips together at Cohen's, we had come a long way from when we were boys. We got caught up with each other's news as much as possible before I had to return to my unit. On saying goodbye, we both wished each other well. We knew that the fight was far from over.

On April 15, 1945, the British army arrived at Bergen-Belsen concentration camp. I had heard something of the German atrocities during my time in Belgium, speaking to the Jewish youth of that city and also hearing about the Germans torturing civilians. But nothing could prepare me for what I saw in that camp. Before I tell you about my experience there, an experience that changed my life, I want to give you a sense of how the British people first heard about it. Traveling with the British forces was one Richard Dimbleby, a BBC version of the American journalist Edward R. Murrow, who broadcast via the radio the scene that greeted him soon after the camp had been liberated. People who heard it tell me that he could barely contain himself, and it created quite a stir as the people began to hear what the Third Reich was all about.

> *Here, over an acre of ground lay dead and dying people. You could not see which was which. . . . The living lay with their heads against the corpses and around them moved the awful ghostly procession of emaciated, aimless people, with nothing to do and with no hope of life, unable to move out of your way, unable to look at the terrible sights around them. . . . Babies had been born here, tiny wizened that could not live. . . . A mother driven mad, screamed at a British sentry to give milk to her child, and thrust the tiny mite into his arms, then ran off crying terribly. He opened the bundle and found the baby had been dead for days.*

This day at Belsen was the most horrible of my life.

I spent several weeks at the camp. I was not supposed to, and though I am unlikely to be court-martialed today, if only the major had known what really happened, he would have finally had me for something. But I doubt he could have gotten me much jail time for doing what I did, although technically I was AWOL. The scene was horrific in the camp. There were no gas chambers in Bergen-Belsen, or in any other concentration camp in Germany itself. That form of mass murder was performed in the East, in places like Auschwitz in Poland. But many people died in Bergen-Belsen from starvation and disease, particularly as a result of a terrible typhus epidemic. When I first entered the camp, I met one of the British doctors who were furiously working to save as many of the liberated inmates as possible. I asked him if he needed help, and he told me that he certainly could use some, and so I spent several weeks working with him, day and night. I met many people in my life who have done great things, but this doctor was one of the finest human beings I ever met. He was totally committed to his mission and did everything possible to keep people alive. Sometimes there was nothing to do, and you saw people die right in front of you. If the Nazis represented evil, and surely they did, the doctor (I should add that he was a Gentile) and others like him represented the polar opposite: the goodness and kindness the human species is capable of.

This was more than just a humanitarian mission for me. It was a couple of weeks that would change my life. I had the opportunity to see the dead, some buried in mass graves, the dying, but also the living. I was full of resolve. The concentration camp represented more than just another chapter in the sad history of the persecution of the Jewish people. I felt that if we did not do something, this would never end. I said to myself that this could not go on forever. The only way to stop any more Bergen-Belsens in the future is for us to have our own state, with our own Jewish army to protect us. Though I had spent many years in Habonim and on the Farm, where I dreamt of being a chalutz. *I made the decision to go to Israel because of the couple of weeks I had spent in Bergen-Belsen. Seeing that camp was more powerful than a Bialik poem, a Weizmann speech or the words of Theodore Herzl himself.*

So I said goodbye to the doctor and headed back to my unit. When I returned, the major was fuming and demanded to know where I had been. I told him that I had gotten lost and separated from the unit, and in the mass of confusion that was the end of the war, this same thing had happened to literally thousands and thousands of servicemen. He could not prove I had gone AWOL, which in fact was actually the case, and my friend the doctor had simply not said anything

A view of the Bergen-Belsen concentration camp after the liberation of the camp. Bergen-Belsen, after April 15, 1945

to anyone in authority about what I was doing. Everyone just figured I was where I was supposed to be, and in a manner of speaking, I had been.

Since I knew that I was going to be seeing all kinds of Jewish survivors and ultimately displaced persons, I made a request of the Zionist organization to send me cartons of cigarettes, which I began to distribute. There was a reason for the cigarettes. They represented real currency in those days. It was like handing out money. They could be traded for food, clothing, or any other staple a person needed. I never imagined that passing around cartons of cigarettes would eventually get me in hot water, but I was mistaken. One day the major called me into his office. "Nathan," he said, "I hear that you have been receiving cartons of cigarettes, and since I know that you don't smoke, you must be selling them on the black market. What do you have to say for yourself?"

"Sir," I said, "it is true, I have been receiving cigarettes, and the major is quite right, I do not smoke. Instead, I am passing them out to civilians that I encounter in an effort to foster goodwill toward the British army." Well, he gave me a look of disbelief. He looked as if he was going to fall through the floor. Of course, I was stretching the truth a bit about goodwill, but it sounded pretty good. You have to remember that black marketeering was rampant at the time, and there were men who were making a king's ransom selling cigarettes. Perhaps the notion of black market profiteering was confirming some of the major's prejudices, but as he dismissed me he gave me a look which said, "Sooner or later, I am going to court martial you, Nathan!"

Sooner came in the form of a minor traffic accident I was involved in. I was driving a truck in Brussels, and due to the very narrow streets there, I scratched a private bus. It was just a nick, and considering all the damage that the war had brought, it had to be considered the mildest of casualties. The bus's owner was a crafty fellow, and he must have seen the deep pockets of the British army (not really all that deep at the time) as an opportunity to make some money. He took his case to the authorities, and ultimately charges of negligent driving were levied against me. Of course, the whole case was ridiculous, but the major would have liked nothing more than to see me rotting in a military prison somewhere. I figured that this was serious business indeed, and in the spirit of the Talmudic sage Hillel, "If I am not for myself who will be for me," I decided that I'd better take a crash course in military jurisprudence. I discovered that if a person's actions were due to an error in judgment, he could not be found guilty at a general court martial. They brought me before an assembled military court, and I walked between two very large sergeants. In such a trial, they take your hat off your head and throw it to the floor, which is supposed to be a sign of disgrace. When it came time for me to testify, I told the court that I had merely scratched the bus, and I was terribly sorry, but it was all the result of an error of judgment, and that my driving history would show that up until this time, I had a perfect record. The court found me innocent, and that was that. It felt very good to be free or nearly so, and it would be some time before I would see a jail cell again, but I would see one in good time.

The events that I have been describing took place in Belgium immediately after the war. The Germans had surrendered on May 8, and we had been ordered to Vilvoorde, near Brussels. We had massive pieces of armour and other types of equipment with us, which now that the war was over, were no longer needed. These needed to be sent back to England, so we would take them apart and pack them for shipping. Operation Overlord had been a smashing success. To achieve our victory, we had gone through the largest, most extensive mobilization in Britain's history. Now we were demobilizing. The men in the unit were relieved and anxious to return to their former lives. I had not gotten my demobilization orders yet, but felt that with the combination of the major still being after me over the cigarettes and the fact that I wanted to help the many Jews who were survivors or otherwise displaced persons, the time was ripe for my discharge. I contacted my old buddy, Jack Friedman from Manchester, who had been assigned to Division Headquarters. Jack was a master at getting things through channels fast. He listened to my situation, and told me he would arrange everything within a few weeks time. As usual, Jack was good to his word.

CHAPTER SIX

Illegal Immigration and the Exodus

Before my discharge and while still in Belgium, I had stopped for a meal at one of the many restaurants the British army had set up to accommodate its troops. There, while enjoying a cup of tea and what passed for crumpets, I heard the distinctive sound of Hebrew spoken without the benefit of an English accent. I glanced at the table where the talking was coming from, and found a group of about seven or eight fellows engaged in animated conversation. Not being a shy type, I went over and introduced myself. As the only Jew in my unit, it was refreshing to meet other Jews. It turned out that the fellows were members of the Jewish Brigade, and we soon became fast friends. Just like my experiences at Bergen-Belsen, it would prove to be a transforming event in my life. While we were both fighting for king and country, as it were, the Brigade had a unique history. Though it was a part of the overall British forces, it fought under the flag of the Star of David and was composed of Jews, mostly from Palestine, although any Jew could join. There was precedent for forming such a brigade, as there were similar units throughout the British forces of native soldiers from many of the territories that made up the Empire at the time.

In Brussels with fellows from the British army and the Jewish Brigade.
Left to right: Yitchak Berman, Jack Friedman, Zami Ben Zvi, me,
and a whole group of friends. The occasion was my 22nd birthday
and I could not have spent it with a better group of guys.
(Courtesy of Zami Ben Zvi)

Some of those in the Jewish Brigade had previously served in various units of the British army such as the Palestine Regiment, which had been formed early in the war and had been intended to include both Jewish and Arab volunteers from the Holy Land. This held particular appeal to the British since the Arab leader at the time, the Grand Mufti of Jerusalem, was supporting Hitler, and spent the war years in Berlin, helping to raise an SS unit made up entirely of Muslims. Particularly in light of the information on massacres and mass murders of Jews, there was growing pressure to set up an all-Jewish brigade, and Churchill, after not receiving any objection from Roosevelt, finally set up such a brigade. Late in 1944, the Brigade became active. Brigadier General Ernest Benjamin, an experienced officer of Canadian extraction, and Jewish to boot, was its commander. Besides Benjamin, believe it or not, a Rothschild, London's own Eddy Rothschild who later became a famous horticulturalist, was a major in the unit.

Illegal Immigration and the Exodus

The Jewish Brigade was transferred to Belgium after the fighting, just as my unit had been. The higher ups in the British army were anxious to get them out of Germany, and were worried about Brigade members taking matters into their own hands when it was discovered what the Nazis had done to our people. It was rumored that the Brigade had formed assassination squads after the war to hunt down Nazi war criminals who were in hiding, although I have no first-hand knowledge of this. But as I got to know these fellows—and they were terrific guys—now that the war was won, they told me what they were up to. The main focus of their postwar activities involved helping those who had survived the war. There were in Europe at the time thousands and thousands of Holocaust survivors, most of whom had made it through the concentration and labor camps, but some had been in hiding or spent the war fighting with partisan or resistance units.

The first thing I did for these fellows in the Brigade was to smuggle some of them into Germany and into the newly set up Displaced Persons camps. The idea of getting these Jewish boys into the camps was to buoy the spirits of the survivors. Eventually, when we wanted to help the Jews out of the camps, we used trucks and our familiarity with the camps, as well as the fact that the brigade members were very familiar with the British army. This would all prove to be an enormous benefit.

These fellows from the Brigade were transitioning from their wartime duties; in fact, they would soon be demobilized into working as part of the newly reconstructed *Mossad LeAliyah Bet*. In English, this translates as the Institute for the Second Immigration. In fact, the illegal immigration known as *Aliyah Bet* had actually begun in 1934. Its purpose had been to get the Jews out of Europe amidst growing anti-Semitism, and continued to operate on through the very beginning of the war. It discontinued its activities during the war because it was impossible to get anyone out with the Nazi stranglehold on Europe, but now that the Germans were defeated, *Aliyah Bet* faced a new challenge.

Discharged from the army, I went back to England. Back at the Farm, I met a representative from the Jewish Agency and informed him that I was anxious to return to Europe and work on *Mossad LeAlliyah Bet.* He told me that he had just sent a group from the Farm to do that sort of work, and if I could help out on the Farm for a few months until he could find suitable replacements, he would arrange everything. I agreed. My siblings were not necessarily pleased at the turn of events. First of all, they were glad to have me and Sid back home, and were grateful that we survived the war. Since I did not speak much of my activities in Europe, they became concerned that I had fallen in with a more radical bunch called *Lechi*, otherwise known as the Stern Gang.

Lechi had been accused of the assassination of Lord Moyne, the British High Commissioner of Palestine, in Cairo in 1944, which had caused a tremendous stir back in England and even enraged no less a friend of the Jews than Mr. Churchill himself. Many mainstream Zionists did not approve of their methods to gain Jewish statehood. I assured my family that I had nothing to do with *Lechi*, in fact, the organization that I was aligned with was affiliated with the Haganah, and then I said goodbye as I left for Europe. This was painful, as I knew I would not see my family for some time, but it was the price to be paid for doing this type of work. Later, my siblings would inform me that Scotland Yard would come around to the house every so often and inquire about my whereabouts, and my family would respond that they had no idea where I was, which was true. I did keep a post office box in Paris, where they could get in touch with me, and I would journey to Paris every so often to pick up my mail, always taking a different route and walking around the post office a few times to make sure I was not being followed.

The first thing I was asked to do was to give up my passport. Presumably, there was an Alfy Nathan walking around Europe somewhere, but he was not me. I was, for all intents and purposes, a man without papers, a different kind of displaced person. I did not use an alias as some did. People called me Alfy or Avraham. During this time it was relatively easy to just sink into the woodwork that was

Continental Europe. There were so many people in Europe going to and fro throughout the period of 1945-1948. There were tumultuous political changes, as maps of the continent were being redrawn for the second time in less than thirty years. There were thousands of servicemen in and out of uniform, many in the process of demobilization. Relief workers were present in large numbers also, representing all the major international groups, as well as representatives of Jewish organizations. Of course, there was no shortage of intelligence agents representing all the major powers of Europe, as well as our own people. Our organization was headed by Shaul Avigur, a talented spymaster and organizer of whom it was once said, "Shaul was at once invisible and ever present," and he managed to imbue great loyalty in all of his subordinates. That is not to say that the Mossad had such a tight bureaucratic structure. What seems amazing in hindsight was that the whole enterprise lacked much formal structure, and even though Shaul was at the top and people would often use the expression, "Shaul said so" when demanding something or another, the Mossad lacked an elaborate chain of command. It is true that the people on the boats were officially in the *Palyam*, the navy of the Haganah, but while still in Europe they were under the Mossad. It was all like so many other things that would characterize the soon to be created Jewish state, tremendously informal. Somehow, it all seemed to work.

We rented chateaus all over France and Italy, which were readily available for the right price after the war. We needed such large quarters because we used them to temporarily house the immigrants until we were ready to get them aboard the ships. In the barn we stored supplies, and since I was constantly going back and forth from the chateau, it seemed a likely spot to bed down. There was a lovely French couple who served as caretakers, and they were both very friendly and made me feel at home. I created a room for myself in one corner of the barn by making two walls using boxes filled with canned pineapples to give myself some privacy. While it was not exactly the Ritz, it served me nicely. I got a metal frame and mattress and had a room. And if the police happened to search the barn, they would not suspect anyone was quartered there since I had completely enclosed it. It was a nice haven, and as usual, I could relax with a good book and take myself to a different time and place.

My end of things can best be described in military terms as logistics and supply. We needed to feed and even clothe a large number of people. We needed a place to house the immigrants until they were ready to be transported to the ship. We needed to outfit the ship with whatever equipment and materials it needed. Though there were hundreds of us running around Europe doing all these things, we did not acknowledge each other as we went about our jobs. When I walked the streets of Marseilles and I saw friends from the organization, I would just walk right by them as if they were not there. We knew we were being watched constantly by the French as well as the British. In effect, it can best be described as one big cat and mouse game.

Many of the French were sympathetic to what we were doing. Many French had a strong hostility to their British allies, and were probably gaining some genuine pleasure from our challenging and occasionally frustrating the mighty British Empire. Just as the British had been given their mandate of Palestine in the wake of World War One, so the French had mandates in both Lebanon and Syria. The events of World War Two forced independence, and led to the French being thrown out of those countries. They were none too happy about this, and resented losing their sphere of influence in the Middle East while the British maintained theirs. There were clearly others among the French who did not care one way or another, and were happy to take some fresh, crisp francs to look the other way. Fortunately, the French are a relatively easy group of people to bribe. Of course, the British were putting enormous pressure on them to curtail our activities, so it was imperative that we be kept informed when the heat was on and a raid of some sort was imminent. One of the pressure points was the illegal radio station we maintained in Marseilles.

Illegal Immigration and the Exodus

The illegal radio station was key not only for our ability to communicate between those of us on shore and our people on the ship, it also allowed us to monitor the British navy, who were dead set to stop us before we could reach the coast of Israel. Little did the British know that the person running our radio station was none other than Meir Raines, who would later become a member of Kfar Hanassi. Meir had been a radio officer with the British Fleet, having served with distinction in the Pacific Theater. He knew the British codes backwards and forwards, and therefore could decipher them quickly and get the information back to the ship's captains in the hopes that they could counter the British. The Haganah ran a course to train the radio operators, teaching them Morse code and radio operation, and these folks were called Gideonim. About a third of the Gideonim were women, and one of them, Marga Goren, had come to England with the Kindertransport. She and her husband Uri, who she met through Mossad activities in Marseilles, would become good friends of mine. Marseilles was not a single, isolated station, but rather part of an entire network, as we also operated in Paris, Milan, Rome, Bucharest, and Prague. In addition, all the radio crews on the ships were our people, who communicated not only with the radio stations in Marseilles but with our home stations in Palestine.

The organization trusted me with thousands of francs. There were rumors of a few unscrupulous types who had siphoned off funds they had been entrusted with, but I never witnessed that. Even if a person is not an outright crook, considering we were not being compensated for our activities, perhaps they may have felt they were entitled to skim a little off the top. Thank God, I was never tempted. To people like Uri Goren and myself, the funds were viewed as being endowed with a holy purpose. It was facilitating getting the Jews into the land of Israel, so it was important to make sure the funds were being spent wisely, including what was spent on bribes. I also made sure when I negotiated for the supplies that I got the best price. Yes, I would go to the baker

On the busy streets of Marseilles, circa 1947, while
hard at work for the organization.
(Courtesy of Uri and Marga Goren)

for loaves of bread, and sometimes he would bake through the night to accommodate a large group we had coming in, to the egg man for the eggs, the milk guy, and so on. The fruit and vegetable man was a particular favorite of mine, and when I would come by, he would smile and greet me, "Monsieur Alfy, it is so good to see you. What can I get for you?" He knew that his ship had come in whenever one of ours was due to depart. After all, where else could he find such a good customer? We needed enormous amounts of food, for we needed to be able to feed the people while they were waiting to get on the ship, and then we needed to be able to provide sufficient calories for their journey to Israel.

THE EXODUS

Our biggest challenge in all this business was in coming up with ways of beating the British blockade. They had a tradition as the world's greatest navy and though we were highly motivated, we were still something of a ragtag organization. We used any vessel we could get our hands on, outfitted it with a crew, and tried our best to evade the British attempts on the Mediterranean and along the coast of Israel, and the British were doing their damnedest to try to stop us. The Royal Navy had allocated considerable resources, some thirty naval vessels in all to this task, and the blockade was very tough on us. Churchill had been defeated after the war and the Conservative Party was thrown out of office. Can you imagine that they threw Churchill out after saving the country from the worst national disaster since the Norman invasion? Well, they did, and Clement Atlee took over, which was not good for us. (Atlee had been known for his modesty, and when someone mentioned this fine quality, particularly in contrast to his predecessor, Churchill was said to have remarked of his modesty, "He has a great deal to be modest about.") Perhaps the worst part about Atlee for us was that he appointed Ernest Bevin, the former Minister of Labour, as the new Foreign Minister. Bevin was a miserable sort, an anti-Semite

Exodus ship following British takeover.

who had been the architect of the internment camps in Cyprus. He was totally committed to making sure that no more than the quota of 1,500 Jews per month entered Palestine, and he approached his task with an almost religious like zeal. In addition to the internment camps in Cyprus, there was also the one operating south of Haifa named *Attlit.* Our leadership felt the only way to break the internment strategy was to send ever larger vessels, which, if captured, would overwhelm the internment camps and therefore create a crisis that would force the British hand on immigration. Before, we had generally used smaller ships, sometimes launching two at the same time, in the hopes that one could make it through the blockade. By the spring of 1947, the organization had identified a ship large enough to do the trick.

The *SS President Warfield* was a large steamer, over 320 feet long, and had been built in the 1920s. An American ship, during its heyday it had carried both freight and passengers between Baltimore and Norfolk, Virginia, and ironically, had been used by the British as a training ship during the war before it was returned to the Americans, where it was commissioned as a United States naval vessel. It was decommissioned after the war, and a Baltimore shipwrecking company headed by a fellow named Shorty Levin bought it intending to turn it into scrap, as was done with many of the newly decommissioned ships after the war. Levin was put in touch with one of the organization's front groups with the non-Zionist sounding name of the Chinese-American Industrial Corporation, who bought the ship for $10,000. Not only would the *President Warfield* not end up on the actual scrap heap, it would not end up in the scrap heap of history at all. It would *make* history.

The *Warfield* took on an American crew made up largely of Jewish volunteers who sailed it across the ocean. Though the British and French knew of its presence and its probable use, we went through our usual cat and mouse game as it travelled to several ports. It ended up in La Spezia in Italy, where all of the work to hollow out the ship so it could hold a large number of immigrants, 4500 in total, was done. I should add that La Spezia is located on the Italian coast, and we used it extensively as a port and staging area during the illegal immigration. It was the site of one of the Mossad's most daring operations, called the La Spezia Affair, which had occurred the previous year, and the city's residents were known to be especially sympathetic to our cause and helped a great deal. Unfortunately, Italy was occupied by British troops, so when it got "hot" in La Spezia, the ship, now renamed the *Exodus*, sailed to the south of France.

The ship arrived in Marseilles with a new skipper, Yitzchak "Ike" Aharonowitz, an unimposing looking kibbutznik from *Sdot Yam*, who had previously served as a captain on a merchant ship. Ike, who passed away only a few weeks after I wrote these words, worked with Yossi Harel, who was a highly experienced operative and had tactical command of the ship. Harel, who passed away in 2008 at the age of 90, was one of the great figures in the history of Israeli intelligence. He learned about commando operations and non-conventional military tactics from the master, David Orde Wingate, the British officer who organized the Special Night Squadrons to protect Jewish communities in Palestine from marauding Arabs. So, with Ike and Yossi, we could not have had two more capable and committed leaders to pull this off.

The ship also had a large number of American Jews among its crew, those who had gotten on the ship in America and stayed with it throughout its ordeal. One of them, Bill Bernstein from San Francisco, was later killed by the British. We also had our people, all volunteers, mixed in with the survivors, some from England. In fact, there were seven people from Habonim who had been recruited from the Farm to help with illegal immigration. One of them was my close friend, Sheila Ben Yehuda. They had been brought over by the organization and joined the immigrants in St. Jerome, and despite the language barrier, they were critical, not only for keeping up the morale of the immigrants and doing so many of the jobs necessary during the journey, but also in communicating with us on shore. Among the Americans there was one Gentile, known as "John the Priest," but who was really a Methodist minister named John Stanley Grauel. He had met Ben-Gurion in New Jersey and transformed into a committed Zionist. He would prove extremely helpful in getting out the story to the world press about the *Exodus*, and he would even testify before the United Nations after escaping British captivity. He is buried in Jerusalem, and is one of the many heroes of the *Exodus*.

Things were getting a bit "hot" in Marseilles, as the local authorities were on to us, and we were told that it would be better to launch the ship from Sete, a smaller town in the south of France adjacent to Montpelier. Since the group we would be boarding was larger than anything attempted, we wanted to avoid suspicion, and we moved them by truck convoy from various locations in smaller groups. We had to prepare food for the journey, and one of the items was hard boiled eggs, two per person. So I had to find 9,000 eggs! Can you imagine walking into a store today, even Costco, and asking for 9,000 eggs? I was able, through a variety of sources to get the eggs, and it seemed like it took us forever to boil them using one very large pot, but eventually we had it done.

The next problem was to get such a large group on board without arousing suspicion. We knew the British would be watching, and we did not want them to know the extent of our group. Our idea was to have the trucks arrive every hour on the hour until everyone was on board. We thought this would fool them, but like many well thought out plans, this one went a bit awry. However it transpired, it appeared as though the entire group of 4,500 was boarding at once. Standing on one end of the gangplank were a British intelligence officer and his French colleague. This French officer was, like many other Frenchmen, not very fond of the British. In effect, you could say, our strategy in all of this was to play the French against the British, and we were obviously not the first in history to try this tactic. I remember well the scene on shore as the immigrants, who believed they would soon be in Haifa, began to board the ship. The English officer was counting in English, the Frenchman in French, and to allay suspicions of my country of origin, I counted in Yiddish. The British continued their pressure on the French, and eventually the French caved in, coming on board and removing a part from the boiler room of the ship, thereby preventing the ship from leaving. We had come too far to let this stop us, and came up with a counter measure. We took a plaster cast of the part and went to a foundry, where they worked through the night to make the part. The part was a valve, and you could say this was my first experience in the valve business. We managed to get back to the ship and put it in place, and the ship was ready to go.

Now there was just one problem on board. The pilot had not yet arrived. (A pilot is a mariner who is specifically trained in navigating a ship out of ports and challenging waterways.) Ike decided to take it upon himself to pull out of the harbor, which was pretty tricky. He hit a sand bank, but the ship's engines were so strong that we managed to push out to sea. The British had three or four naval vessels offshore, and the ships were communicating with each other in code. Meir

Raines was listening to this and relaying the information to Ike on board so they could come up with the best strategy to elude these vessels. Ike managed to do this by maximizing the full thrust and throttle of the *Exodus'* engines, and was now out in the sea. Unfortunately but not unexpectedly, the British ships had radioed the ship's positions to their base in Malta, and before long, what seemed like an armada, including a cruiser and destroyers, was trailing the ship, ramming it violently, and a large party of soldiers, in violation of maritime law as the ship was still in international waters, boarded the ship.

The crew and passengers were not armed, having been restricted by the organization from using any arms on these voyages. They did resist the boarding, throwing boiling cans of vegetables and other foodstuffs such as potatoes at the soldiers, who killed three of our people and wounded a number of others. In all, it was a very bad scene, terribly depressing for the poor survivors as the ship was towed into Haifa harbor. Many are familiar with this saga, even those who did not live through it, because of Leon Uris's book and the subsequent movie that was made starring Paul Newman, whose character was presumably based on Yossi Harel. (I should add that as a witness to the events, as enjoyable as the book and the movie were, Uris takes a great deal of literary license with the story, as several of the facts he presented are not accurate.) From Haifa and against the wishes of the people, the British forcibly transferred the people onto three ships and sent them back to France, in this case back to the south of France, where, of course, we were waiting for them.

We had reasoned that the group was too large for the camps at Cyprus. That was true. But we had not anticipated them being sent back to their port of embarkation. It was as if Bevin was saying to France and other European countries, "You send us your Jews, we will send them right back to you." Somehow, and I am not sure how we managed to pull this off, we got word to the passengers on all three ships that they were not to leave the ships under any circumstances. And when the boats pulled into the harbor, the British told the French that they wanted to unload the people. The French responded that they would only unload those who wanted to be unloaded, refusing categorically to use force against those on board. Only a few of the sick left the ship. This shows the fortitude and spirit of the people, for the conditions were horrible, simply beyond what most healthy people could tolerate, to say nothing of Holocaust survivors, who had already endured so much. Not only were sanitary conditions unspeakable, but it was compounded by the sweltering heat of the middle of the summer.

For the most part, during the period of illegal immigration the British troops behaved decently. This was not necessarily the case with the events around the Exodus, as there was a great deal of violence directed at the crew and survivors. But the plight of the survivors even touched some in uniform. My friend Sheila tells the story that when it was decided that the ships were going to Germany, the survivors, as you can well imagine, were beside themselves. The ship stopped in Gibraltar, and the soldiers on board were relieved by a Scottish contingent that guarded them for a 24-hour period. Two of the soldiers came down into the hold, and just before they left, they handed the people blankets and sweets, and one of them said, "I don't know where you are going and what you are doing, but you have my blessing." Clearly, many of the soldiers disliked the tasks they were assigned, particularly in guarding Holocaust survivors who were now in internment camps in Cyprus and Europe. These were troops who had helped liberate concentration camps and freed Jews, and who were now guarding those same Jews. It defied logic, but in defense of my country of origin, I remember Uri Goren once telling me that we were lucky to be facing the British as adversaries. Things would have been much worse with any other colonial power, and I think that is very true.

In general, those aboard the *Exodus* had initially refused to eat to protest the British refusal to let them into Palestine. They had undergone a 24-hour hunger strike. It became apparent that this standoff would continue for a long time, in fact, the *Exodus* remained in France for three weeks, and the question became who would feed the immigrants. The British flatly refused. Finally, there was an agreement whereby the French Red Cross would feed them, and some of us became members of the French Red Cross. It was the first time in my life I ever wore a uniform with the symbol of a cross. I should add that the ship was not allowed in the port, it stayed out a mile or so. Therefore, we loaded up crates of fruits and vegetables on a barge and pulled that barge out next to the three British vessels that the passengers of the *Exodus* were now staying on. Although I would load the food on the ship, I did not have contact with any of our people on board. Marga Goren, one of our *Gideonim*, was allowed on board since she was dressed as a nurse. Otherwise, we had to get messages inside the crates of food.

We decided to use the vegetable crates, hiding messages in several of the tomatoes. One day, as I was unloading the crates on one of the three ships, I noticed that the troops on board were British paratroopers. I could see the shoulder patches of some of the men, and just my luck, they read 6th Airborne Division. These were the blokes who as part of Operation Tonga had parachuted in ahead of us at Normandy and took out the most powerful of the German artillery batteries so they could not shell us when we landed, but now was not the time to thank them. In fact, I had fought side by side with the men of the 6th during the Battle for Caen. In the event that one of them might recognize me in the south of France from the time we spent together on the northern coast of France just four short years ago, I tried to keep my head turned away. But just when I finished with the unloading, I could feel two eyes peering at me from about twenty paces behind.

Fortunately, we had finished getting everything off the barge and onto the ships, so I figured I would try and keep my back to him and ignore any protocol of saying goodbye. But then I could hear a voice, a raspy and hard-sounding bark that can only emanate from the heavily used vocal chords of a seasoned sergeant major in the British Army yelling, "Corporal, stop that man at once!" As I turned around, I could see a finger pointing at me and the sound of army boots on the move coming my way. I took off as fast I could for the barge, and had to jump several feet off the side onto the barge. It was one of my most athletic moments. Luckily for me, adrenaline made the difference, as I ended up on the barge and not in the sea. I called to the ship towing us to disembark at once, but it was to be the last time I would be allowed on one of the ships. Orders went out not to let me on again, and if I ever tried to, to take me into custody at gunpoint.

The ships eventually went to Germany, housing the people in terrible conditions on the site of a former concentration camp. The British used the excuse that this was the only place with sufficient facilities to accommodate them until it could be decided what to do with the immigrants. But the cruel irony of this decision was not lost on us or on the world at large. It was extremely painful and terribly traumatic for the people on board. We had promised them an end to their suffering through a new life in Eretz Yisrael. Unfortunately, they were back in the country that had caused their misery. Some we managed to smuggle out of Germany, some would end up in the camps at Cyprus being caught again by the blockade, but the vast majority of the 4,500 from the *Exodus* had to wait until late in 1948 or early 1949 to arrive in Israel. But there is no question that the events of the *Exodus* (and one still feels a great bond with everyone who was a player in that episode) were a turning point for the entire cause for statehood and convinced the British that their mandate was effectively at an end.

The success of *Mossad LeAliyah Bet* depended on many things. Obviously, the commitment of those of us in the field was critical. It was fueled by personal wartime experiences and the knowledge of what the stakes were. The people involved were a diverse group. There were Americans, Canadians, and British like me, and of course the many Brigade members and others from Palestine. But as much as the people were critical, without the money we couldn't have done it. We were greatly supported through money raised by the Joint Distribution Committee, known to many of us as the Joint, which raised large sums from the English-speaking world, particularly America. Every dollar given in every drive for funds, whether in Johannesburg, Manchester, or Manhattan, was vital to the operation.

As a bagman entrusted with these funds, I would carry around a suitcase full of francs, and was always on the look-out in a city rife with pickpockets and thieves interested in separating me from my case with the money. I was ready to fight to keep it. Uri Goren, the friend I mentioned earlier who was a member of the Palmach and later a senior officer in the Israeli Army and a member for a time of *Kfar Hannasi*, was working for the organization at the time, and he would get the money, sometimes as much as 20,000 or 30,000 francs at a time, depending on how many people I had to pay, and transfer it to me. When walking around with that kind of money, I tried to look as natural as possible, as if there was nothing special in that case. You just try to blend in and not generate interest from anyone. Well, one night I was in a taxi making my rounds to pay the various suppliers, when there appeared a large number of police on the street. They were stopping every taxi on the boulevard, and I told the driver that if he could get around the police somehow, I would make it worth his while. It soon became clear that it was impossible to bypass the police. Apparently, there had been a murder in Marseilles that night, and they believed the murderer had fled in a taxi. When they pulled me out of the taxi and began to question me, the suitcase full of francs aroused their suspicion, and within minutes I was in handcuffs and on my way to the police station.

I had been instructed by the organization that if I was ever caught not to say anything, to keep my mouth shut at all times. Don't use your mouth for eating or drinking either, they told me, as I could be drugged with something that would make me prone to talk. (Loose lips sink ships could never have been more apropos.) This, for anyone accused of a crime, is sound advice, for talking can only get you in trouble. It is hard to incriminate anyone, yourself included, when you say nothing.

Illegal Immigration and the Exodus

The organization had told me that if I was locked up, they would eventually get me out, and that I just needed to hang in there and be patient. The last time I had seen a jail cell was when I was locked up for a night prior to the court martial while still in the army. But that is a military affair, and while not exactly enjoyable, it was nothing compared to being locked up with common criminals. It was extremely depressing to be incarcerated, because you can look out and see freedom, but those metal bars are unyielding. They are a barrier to all the wonderful freedoms one takes for granted, that is, until you lose them.

As bad as it may have seemed, the several days I spent within the confines of the Marseilles jail were quite educational. As tight-lipped as I was, my eyes and ears were both wide open. There were several dozen characters locked up with me over several days. They were quite a bunch. It was if that famous line of Claude Rains from the movie *Casablanca*, "Round up the usual suspects," had actually come to life. In my cell were several pickpockets, burglars, and one man who had been accused of extortion, and another charged with attempted murder. There was the usual drunk who the police seemed to have particular contempt for, having dragged the fellow into the large cell to be abused by all. For most of the chaps in with me, this was not their first stay in a jail cell, nor from all appearances was it likely to be their last.

For the first night I was there we were all in a holding cell, men and women together. Perhaps the most colorful people were the ladies of the evening, who were not ladies in the usual sense. Though I had heard plenty of strong language in my day and knew a little French, it did not take a linguist to get the gist of what they were saying. They were bloody mad at the authorities, and I again suspected it was either a matter of money or perhaps exchanging some free services in lieu of their release. But in any event, once they saw me and heard I was found with a suitcase full of money, they determined that I might be a potential client. I neglected to inform them that the money was not mine to spend. I suppose they figured that since they were losing a night of work, they were at least going to try to make some money to make up for it. The several ladies present, who were street prostitutes dressed in their tight dresses and high heels and wearing strong, almost noxious perfume to boot, were like something out of a late night movie. They did not seem to think solicitation in the Marseilles police station was somehow a bit too forward, and with a mixture of charm and persistence that emphasized their superior ability to ply their craft, they were after me the whole night. I managed to resist, and by the next day I was in a cell with only men.

The French were trying their best to get me to talk. They questioned me without success, and thought they would make an impression on me as I waited outside the interrogation room. They were working over a thief who would not provide information about his associates in a stolen tire ring. It was clear that they were punching and kicking him about the body, as he was groaning from the pain. Eventually, two policemen, each carrying him by the elbows, took him back to his cell because he could not walk on his own, his legs having grown rubbery with the beating. When I saw him later, he told me what they had done, but when I asked to see the bruises, they were not there. Had this all been a fake show just to scare me? Apparently not, because it was clear he was in real pain, but I only found out years later in Israel from some friends who were interrogators that there are certain places where you can hit a person so he will not bruise. Fortunately, I never experienced this on my own person because they decided not to rough me up, and eventually I was released. I was glad to be out, and since no one in the organization asked about my stay, I didn't ask how they had secured my release.

One of the most interesting missions during the time I spent in France was when we were assigned to get a group of 600 young women, all displaced persons who were in a camp in Sweden, on a ship that would travel the North Sea along the Atlantic Coast and enter the Mediterranean Sea through the Straits of Gibraltar. Given the gender of the passengers, we would no doubt have little difficulty getting volunteers to serve on the crew for the voyage. We had another problem.

Since we had never taken that route, we did not have a good map of the North Sea. It was decided that I should go back to England and acquire one.

How to get back to England? There was a Canadian freighter docked in Marseilles harbor, and I assumed the identity of one of the officers on the ship. Fortunately, no one asked me any questions about ice hockey, and I made it in. I then contacted my friend Michael Cohen, who I had known from Habonim and was an officer in the British Navy. (His brother, Joseph Cohen, was a prominent physician who worked for the organization and was aboard the Exodus as its medical doctor.) He was extremely smart, having served as code breaker in the super secret Ultra project in Bletchley Park during the war. I asked him, "Michael, can you help me?" and he agreed, and took me to a store that specialized in cartography and carried the type of maps we were interested in. He indicated the right ones, given the route we planned on taking, and after thanking him, I was ready to go back to France the next day.

I was under express orders not to contact any members of my family while in England. While I did not do that, I could not take my mind off them. I decided to walk by their house. It was nighttime, and I had disguised myself a bit so if they happened to come upon me by accident, they would not recognize me. I got near enough to the house and walked around the neighborhood. Eventually, I saw the lights on in the house, and to me this seemed to signal that all was in order. It was enormously comforting, but, thank God, I was able to maintain the discipline of not getting any closer, although I suppose the organization would not have been pleased in the least if they had found out that I managed to get as close as I did.

I now had to worry about getting the maps out of England. I took two suitcases, one with all my clothes in it and the other one with the maps covered by towels and other things designed to hide them. The customs official, a tall, rail thin chap whose super serious-looking official expression never wavered in the few minutes I was in his company, caught my eye, and he stopped me. He instructed me to open the suitcase. My heart started to beat very fast and I tried to stop sweating, but my undershirt was beginning to feel moist as I opened the suitcase. Both of the cases were nearly identical, and, given the stress of the situation, I suddenly forgot which of the suitcases the maps were in. I began to unzip the case he had pointed to, and was never so happy to see my trousers, shirts, and stockings in all my life. The official seemed satisfied with what he saw and told me to go on my way. I was plenty relieved. Had he picked the other suitcase, it could have been more than a little hairy.

1947 was a critical year for us. Despite the fact that the Jews of the *Exodus* were sent back to Europe and would not arrive in the Holy Land until 1948, the mission had been successful in that it was a great public relations victory for us. World opinion was moving in our direction, and it became clear that the British could not keep the Jews out of Palestine. The British were still there, but they made their intentions clear that they were abandoning their mandate, and the United Nations was busy coming up with a plan that would satisfy both us and the Arabs, with particular emphasis on the latter. The partition plan would be approved in November, but several months earlier I went to speak with Tuvia, one of the leaders of the organization. I knew little about him, or even if Tuvia was his real name. I told him that after two years of this covert type of activity, I was anxious to go overt and head to Palestine to help build what we all hoped would be a state. He told me that he would get back to me in several days. Later, when we met in a seaside café with both of us reading newspapers, sipping coffee, and pretending to look at the calm waves of the sea, Tuvia, in his *sabra*-accented English, gave me the go-ahead.

Since I did not have a passport, I was given an address in Marseilles. I ended up in an apartment where the organization ran its documents division. There I met a lovely young woman named Shulamit who did not fit the stereotype of a forger, whatever that may happen to be, but was very skilled at her craft. She told me to take the passport and the accompanying information, which contained the vital statistics about where I had grown up and went to school and who my relatives were. I memorized all the pertinent data as if I were preparing for an appearance on some radio quiz show. I was ready to answer any questions the Mandate authorities would no doubt ask when I entered Palestine. (I should add that, like all others who had come over like this, I handed the passport back to the organization as soon as I arrived, and it would be some time before I would get one under my own name. Obviously many people had come over in this manner so this was not at all unusual.) I had a week to wait before I could get passage on a ship, so I took my first real holiday in a long time, spending a week enjoying the sites of Monaco. It would be a long time before I would take another holiday.

PART THREE

In Israel at Last

CHAPTER SEVEN

The Founding of Kfar Hanassi

"On July 2 a new kibbutz was founded, overlooking the River Jordan and facing the Syrian Heights. It was only five miles from the area held by the Syrian forces who had seized Mishmar Ha-Yarden. The kibbutz was named Kfar Ha-Nasi (President's Village) in honour of Chaim Weizmann. It was made up of members of the Habonim youth movement who had been preparing for months to set up a kibbutz in this area. Most of them came from England and Australia. A week after their kibbutz was established, its members found themselves in the centre of a battle as Syrian troops broke the truce in an attempt to seize the western side of the River Jordan, that ran half a mile beyond the kibbutz boundary. But the Syrians were driven off, and the slow, hard, patient work of construction began, within sights of the Syrian machine-gun posts on the facing hills to the east."

—From *Israel, A History* by Sir Martin Gilbert, p. 210

I arrived in the port of Haifa on the passenger ship, the *Caronia*. I proceeded to make my way through the gauntlet of Mandate immigration officials who greeted me. If you remember, I had received from

Shulamit, the organization's master forger, a passport. I may have neglected to mention that its origin was Canadian. I had memorized all of the pertinent information as instructed and with my best contrived Canadian accent, proceeded to answer the standard questions to the satisfaction of the officials. I then met a member of the organization at a predetermined locale and handed the passport to him. I was Canadian no more. I then reunited with my Habonim group, some of whom had begun streaming into Palestine in the past year. Others, like me, had been working in illegal immigration in France and Italy.

Soon after I arrived in 1947, the British came to the conclusion that Palestine was essentially ungovernable. They deferred to the United Nations as to what its political future should be. Our representatives came to the United Nations to argue the cause of Jewish statehood, just as they had been doing since the days of Theodore Herzl. Arab leaders put forth the case against a Jewish state, as many still do today. Other leaders spoke as well. One seemed to sum up our cause rather well:

"The Jewish people have been closely linked with Palestine for a considerable period in history. As a result of the war, the Jews as a people have suffered more than any other people. The total number of the Jewish population who perished at the hands of the Nazi executioners is estimated at approximately six million. The Jewish people were therefore striving to create a state of their own, and it would be unjust to deny them that right." I should add that the eloquent speaker was none other than Andrei Gromyko, and the nation he represented, the Soviet Union.

The United Nations authorized a partition plan. The plan called for two separate states, one Jewish and one Arab, with Jerusalem under international control. Though our state would be a small one, our leaders accepted it. The Arabs rejected it outright and there began a great deal of rioting and violence against Jews by the Arab population. Our group was at the time staying at Kfar Blum, named for the French Socialist Jewish political leader, Leon Blum. It was also known as the

The Founding of Kfar Hanassi

Anglo-Baltic kibbutz since its founding members were composed of British, American and South African Habonim members as well as those from Baltic countries.

Kfar Blum is located in the Galilee's Hula Valley. The first settlement in the area, Yesod Ha'Maala, went back to the 1880s and the First Aliyah. Gradually, more settlements came into existence. There was one road which ran through the valley and at its starting point there was a very large sign that read, "Do not stop for the next 40 miles." The reason was that the Hula was a swampland and there were big problems with malaria. When you went out at night, you had to be very careful and make sure you were completely covered in clothing. It did not matter how hot and humid it was. If you contracted the disease, it could be very nasty indeed.

My truck driving skills however were put to immediate use during those days. When I drove, I had to be careful not to interact with any of the British soldiers who were still in the country. If they had found out who I was, they would have taken me in straight away. I would drive a Mack truck, hauling fruit to Haifa or milk down to Deganya. In the city of Rosh Pina, the British had erected a customs barrier. They had done this during the period when France had a mandate over Syria and Lebanon. Being in Rosh Pina allowed the British to collect tariffs for goods that travelled between Palestine and Syria as well as those that travelled between Jordan and Syria.

It was the intention of our small group to live the kibbutz life fully. The only question that remained to be decided was whether we should join an existing kibbutz or establish our own. The body most responsible for making such a decision was the Jewish Agency, which, at the time, was serving as the representative body of the Jewish community in Palestine. In October, 1947, it was decided that we should move to the city of Hadera, as a precursor to starting our own settlement.

Hadera offered the opportunity of earning money. Our primary source of income was derived from working in the fish ponds and fruit orchards that were plentiful in the area. We were what you would refer to today as "day laborers." To find out where we would be working the following day, one member of our group would go down to the local labor office.

We had stiff competition in the local labor market. It came from Arab laborers who were willing to work for cheaper pay than we were. Not that our compensation was what one would call extravagant. It was the equivalent of $1.50 a day. One farmer was accepting only Arab labor. Though he was Jewish, he was also a capitalist and as such was interested in minimizing his labor costs. We were not at all pleased with his attitude and felt he needed a little persuading to see things our way. We came to his home and told him that if he knew what was good for him, he would hire us. Apparently, he was convinced that we were serious people and, by the next day, we were picking his oranges.

We rode to work in Egged buses. The buses were old Fords with a chassis. They built a bus on the back of it. The buses were so crowded that we would frequently ride on the outside, hanging on for dear life. When the bus slowed down, we would extend our arms on to the orange groves and pick a couple of oranges. That was our breakfast. When I first came to America in 1976, I would occasionally saunter into a supermarket and make my way over to the produce department. My eyes would always light up when Jaffa oranges were in season. I would buy a bunch not only for their sweet taste but because they reminded me of those breakfasts on the back of the bus. Today, Israel produces very few Jaffa oranges, but in those days they could be found in great abundance. I would travel to Herut Bet between Hadera and Netanya and pick oranges for the Americans who had founded a moshav there. My big treat in those days, after a long day of picking fruit, was indulging in a seltzer drink. These were in the days before Coke and other soda brands were common in the country. The Israelis called the seltzer drink Gazoz, which was basically a fruity-tasting syrup mixed with carbonated water. It was a kind of national beverage. Boy, it sure tasted good.

The Founding of Kfar Hanassi

Several of us took temporary work assignments on other kibbutzim that needed workers. I was one of them and headed to Kiryat
Anavim. It is a fairly old kibbutz located in the Judean hills about 10
miles west of Jerusalem. As the name of the kibbutz (city of grapes)
suggests, grapes along with other fruit were a mainstay of agricultural
life there. The work conditions were not the best. We would take big
compressors, like the kind that you would use to break up concrete,
dig a hole and put in earth, then compost, manure and finally plant
a plum tree. The problem was what we would find the next morning.
It would not be uncommon for the local Arabs to have uprooted the
entire enterprise. You felt great frustration knowing that the previous
day's work had been for naught.

Kiryat Anavim was the first kibbutz to be established in the Judean
hills. It was of immense strategic importance due to its close proximity
to Jerusalem. Kibbutz members were Eastern European in origin, having come to Palestine in various waves during the 1920s. We communicated with them by employing a mishmash of Yiddish and Hebrew.
One thing we learned about our hosts was that they had an aversion
to potatoes. When we would gather in the dining hall for Friday night
dinner, the potatoes had magically found their way to our table. It was
fine with us because we were good and hungry and would have eaten
just about anything.

One food we rarely got to enjoy were apples. Though the kibbutz
had apple orchards and we spent plenty of hours picking them, that
was as close as we got to enjoying them. I should clarify that by saying
we were allowed one apple a week, which seemed to be something of
a pittance given their numbers. The reason was that they represented
cash to the kibbutz and all of the decent apples were sold at market.
The one time I remember the rule being broken was when the United
Nations accepted the Partition Plan. We were awakened in the middle
of the night and gathered in the dining room, singing, dancing, and,
of course, eating as many apples as our stomachs would allow.

As the British prepared to leave in 1948, we were essentially in a state of war with the Arabs. Under the direction of Abd al Qadir al-Husayni, the Mufti of Jerusalem's nephew, a siege was initiated against Jerusalem. The Mufti was the title of the major Muslim leader in the country and in this case he was a rabid anti-Semite who had spent part of World War Two in Berlin where he met with his host, Hitler, on how best to dispose of the Jews of Palestine. The idea was to starve the city and kill anyone who dared break the stranglehold. The British mostly looked the other way, trying to minimize their own casualties before they left. Together with our group at Kiryat Anavim, I was called back to Hadera. The only problem was that traveling was so dangerous that our only viable option was going by armored convoy. What constituted an armored convoy? Not much. The cabins of the trucks that we travelled in were made of two steel plates with stone in between them and no real glass. There were just small slits of glass, just large enough for your eyes to see through. You simply prayed that the Arab snipers, who were poised to fire at us from the high ground where they were positioned, had bad aim.

This was a particularly rough period as the Arabs began indiscriminate shelling of the Jewish neighborhoods of West Jerusalem. Terrible massacres took place. One involved a convoy of Jewish medical personnel that had been dispatched to Hadassah Hospital to help treat the wounded in Jerusalem. In those days, Hadassah Hospital was located on Mount Scopus and was extremely vulnerable to Arab violence. The entire convoy was ambushed and 79 people, mainly doctors and nurses, were killed. The Arabs reasoned, much as they do today, that a strategy of terror would create a sense of fear and demoralization not only in Jerusalem but throughout the entire country. They were wrong.

As you may surmise, we made it to Hadera. It was a harrowing journey to be sure. The most frightening element of all was in not knowing when you are going to come under fire. But we had steely resolve and that seemed to be enough to counteract whatever fear may have resided in us. It was a resolve that I had first felt in my bones when I saw the dastardly scene that was Bergen-Belsen. Now I was drawing on that emotion. We were aiming to put an end to the suffering and bloodshed that encapsulated far too much of our nation's history. We were not going to let the Arabs finish what the Germans had started. Perhaps they would try but we were prepared to give them one hell of a fight.

Many of the points along that fateful Jerusalem–Tel-Aviv road were under the control of some of the best Arab fighters, known as the Arab Legion, which was under the command of veteran British officers. The toughest stretch along that road was in a high ground named Latrun, where they had a base. Several battles were fought in an effort to dislodge the Arabs from Latrun but every attempt failed. Some of our fighters died trying. Though they had great courage, they were no match for the heavy guns, many British in origin, that the Legion possessed. One approach that we employed was to erect what became known as a "Burma Road" as a way around having to use the main highway. It was a brilliant idea and if you saw the movie "Cast a Giant Shadow," about the life and exploits of Colonel Mickey Marcus, you may remember a scene which featured the construction of that road. Though British artillery and Arab snipers killed some of our road workers, the road became operational by June of 1948. The people of Jerusalem got some relief.

By the time I arrived in Hadera, the British were leaving in large numbers. Statehood was declared on 14 May. It was a joyous day for all. Though there was mandatory conscription of all Jewish inhabitants at the time, our group was not conscripted. We were none too happy about this development. There was, however, a reason behind it. Plans were in the works for us to set up a kibbutz in a border area. Our group was given two locations. One was the present site of Ramot Meanshe, a village which had been captured by the Irgun during the war and which the Iraqi army was now threatening. The other possibility was in the abandoned Bedouin village of Mansura al-Chait, near

Rosh Pina. Fortunately, we didn't have to worry about the Iraqi army. They were nowhere to be found. Instead, we were going to be facing the full force and might of the Syrian army.

Ben-Gurion had reasoned that our group was ideally suited for such a settlement. Nearly all of us had major combat experience and therefore would be poised to stave off an enemy attack. It is true that facing the German guns in Normandy provided some preparation for facing Arab guns in Mansura al-Chait. The Jewish Agency had provided us with precious few details about the area because travel there was so dangerous. We decided that just as spies had been sent to tour the land in the Bible, we should do likewise. In our case, we went with one spy, Johnny Tena (Tendler). Johnny was a good friend of mine and had been a tailor in London before the war. After we established the kibbutz, Johnny became an expert in chickens. As he got older, he would visit all of the local kibbutzim and give them advice on how to properly raise them. Though he was expert in chickens, he was anything but chicken. He was chosen for the mission because he was fearless. Unlike the spies from the Bible who spoke badly about the land, Johnny came back with an excellent report. Though the area was not inhabited by giants, it was teeming with Syrian troops. Due to the danger, he was able to view the land only from a distance. From a hill he noticed that there were sunflowers blooming all around. We inferred from this that the land was rich and ideal for cultivation. Little did we know that these beautiful sunflowers were wedged in between large rocks and boulders. We would become acquainted with them soon enough.

The land had become available for settlement due to the village leader having taken the entire population to Syria during the fighting. There was also another nearby Bedouin village that stayed put during the war. Its name was Tuba. They would be our new neighbors. By June 11 a truce had been declared during the War of Independence, and this gave us the perfect opening.

HABONIM
PIPE PRODUCTS LTD

Industrial Park, Rosh Pina-Hatzor,
P.O.Box 72, Rosh Pina 12000, Israel.
Tel: 069-35222. Tlx: 6795 HBNIM.
Fax: 069-36005.

Date: 19.3.89

Our Ref:

To :   Sharon   U.S.A.

Att: Alfy

On July 2nd 1948 large tractor came from Kfar Giladi to open the path to the new settlement at Mansura el cheit.

Name of settelment   : Kfar Hanassi.

Name of Tractor driver : Alfy Natan.

Best wishes, Purim Sameach.

Colin Primost

This letter was sent to me from the kibbutz nearly 41 years after the founding of the kibbutz. July 2, 1948, remains for me a memorable date.

We gathered during the evening of July 1 at the Kibbutz Machanaim, near the former British air base. The way new settlements were set up would be that each of the kibbutzim would lend you four or five people, a truck, and digging materials. Since the legality of the settlement could always be challenged, we would gather at nightfall and be finished by early morning. When I say finished, I mean that tents would be set up, barbed wire installed, and perhaps most importantly, trenches dug. The real work would begin after our fellow kibbutzniks had left by 6:00 A.M.

Forty of us were left to defend the kibbutz. How did we do it? Did we have a garrison of weapons upon which to draw? Not exactly. We started out with one revolver. To make the Syrians think we had considerably more firepower, we would run around at night firing the gun from various points in the settlement. The truce was soon over, but the Syrians never launched a full assault against us. To this day, I still do not understand why. There is no question in my mind they could have easily overwhelmed us. The kibbutz, like the state of Israel itself, seemed to survive in those years on a combination of guts, luck, and a healthy dose of Divine Intervention.

Along with the truce came a contingent of United Nations peace-keeping forces. They were there to enforce the truce and included Belgian, Swedish, American, and French soldiers. Shortly after we moved in to Mansura, some of these forces paid us a social visit. They told us that our settlement was a violation of the truce agreement and ordered us to take down our tents and vacate the area immediately. Yitzchak Eder, one of our members who would later serve as the kibbutz archivist, had served with the Belgian army during World War Two and recognized one of the peacekeepers. The man had been his commanding officer during the fighting in that war. It was not a friendly reunion. The two men stared each other down, and Yitzchak could stare you down pretty good. They again told us to leave. We told them we only took orders from our leadership in Tel Aviv. They started to give us a hard time about the trenches we had dug. They wanted to know what they were for and we told them they were for irrigation pipes. They gave us a look which said, "you must be joking" but did nothing. We had a standoff. Fortunately, United Nations peacekeeping troops were about as effective in 1948 as they are today. They had us outgunned but lacked the will to act. They vowed to return, but, in true United Nations form, it proved to be an idle threat.

The Founding of Kfar Hanassi

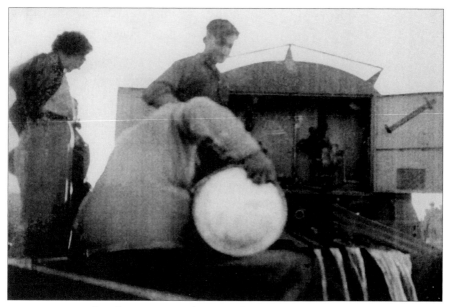

Unloading water after another trip to Rosh Pina.

The first few months of the settlement were very challenging. One of our challenges was in accessing clean water. We had acquired an old gasoline tanker courtesy of the British army, who after leaving the country had left some heavy machinery and equipment behind. We took the tanker, cleaned it out, and I would drive it down to Rosh Pina and fill it up with water. We also set up a primitive shower. We put up a wall made out of sacking and placed a tripod made of wood, and an old seven-pound cucumber can with holes punched in functioned as the spout. Someone would stand on a crate and serve as the water pourer for those enjoying the shower below.

One night we were anticipating an attack from the Syrians. It was decided that since the truck represented our lifeline, we should take it out of the area. I was to drive it down to Rosh Pina until the danger abated. Just like on my trip from Jerusalem in the convoy, we took precautions. We had reinforced the front window, leaving only the tiny glass slits to see out of, just like on the harrowing trip from Jerusalem. As I began driving into the night, I noticed that the moon was shining brightly, creating reflections all around me. I began to see things, thinking these reflections were Syrian troops who were preparing to fire on me. Finally, the hallucinations were driving me mad. In frustration, I pulled out a hammer and knocked out the entire front window. I now stared directly into the evening air. I was a sitting duck, without any kind of protection. Luckily, I found my way to Rosh Pina.

Though we did not get attacked by the Syrians that night, not every kibbutz in the area had been so lucky. Mishmar Hayarden, a nearby settlement, was one example. They had been the victims of a massive Syrian attack in June of 1948. They held off the initial assault, but several days later the Syrians returned with eight tanks, began a massive artillery barrage and even strafed the area with aircraft. Fourteen brave defenders of the kibbutz were killed in the battle. Twenty were taken prisoner. They were forcibly marched all the way to Damascus and held captive under brutal conditions for thirteen months. I saw them when they returned. It was a sad sight. They had been tortured and were physically and mentally scarred. They were so broken in spirit that it was felt that they could not resume any semblance of a normal life. They were sent to an asylum to recover. I do not know what became of them.

While we knew what would happen if we should be captured by the Syrians, the Arab armies did not have to fear being captured by us. They knew they would receive fair and humane treatment, just as the German soldiers did not have to fear being captured by the British or American forces. In many respects, this worked to our advantage. We had to fight harder because the stakes were so high and the consequences of defeat were simply unthinkable. If we were to lose, God forbid, we knew we were done for. There would be no second chances. When a prominent Arab was asked to explain the Jewish success in the war despite the overwhelming odds it faced, he summed up the situation this way, "We can always retreat. The Jews either would win or die." He was just about right.

One of our greatest problems that we faced was an acute shortage of weaponry. During the time of British rule, their army was constantly raiding our caches and confiscating what few weapons we possessed. No doubt some of these weapons found their way into Arab hands. Perhaps our greatest challenge was in overcoming the arms embargo that existed. It was rigorously enforced on the seas by the British navy. The two ceasefires of 1948 actually benefited us in that they allowed us time to purchase and smuggle into the country large amounts of weapons from Czechoslovakia. The day that we received our first Czech rifles on the kibbutz was like a holiday. Those weapons were really fantastic, very well made indeed. Though there were some who tried to make political hay out of a communist country selling weapons to a left wing Jewish government, there was nothing ideological here. There was no conspiracy. We would have bought weapons from anyone willing to sell them to us. Only the Czechs were willing. They were not motivated by ideology. They needed cash. We needed weapons. It was a perfect match.

In addition to the rifles, we had a small artillery piece. This was in the event that the army could not reach us in time. Otherwise, we were ready with some homemade weapons, including a favorite of irregular forces the world round, the Molotov cocktail. While we were not fortunate like the Arabs to get British arms, we did manage to get some other pieces of equipment that they left behind. At one of their abandoned air force bases, the British had left behind some old Quonset huts. We decided to help ourselves and took them apart, using one to help construct our bakery and the other for our clothing store. That was how we built the kibbutz, scrounging around and being creative. Occasionally this approach backfired on us, as this story told by Gusti Rifind and printed in the Kibbutz fifty year anniversary book illustrates.

Some members of the kibbutz got an idea of 'lifting' a tractor. They persuaded Yitzchak Eder, who coordinated the kibbutz, and he dispatched a unit of five members, armed with a submachine gun. They drove to what they thought was an abandoned Arab village on the Lebanese border together with a member of one of the neighborhood moshavim, who showed the way.

Upon arriving in the village, they found the place full of Arabs and Druze harvesting the fields. The moshavnik spoke with the villagers and told us that they were willing to let us have the tractor, but were concerned about Qawuqji's forces (the Arab Liberation Army set up by Fawzi-al-Qawuqji and composed of volunteers from many Arab countries) active in the area. They suggested that we stage a fight in order to get the tractor. They agreed that the villagers would bring the tractor to the center of the village and the kibbutzniks would fire on them and drive them away.

At first everything went according to plan. The kibbutzniks took positions on the outskirts of the village and the Druze ran away. All of a sudden, the kibbutzniks were barraged with gunfire from all sides. They found themselves in a trap. Minki, the former British officer who commanded the group, ordered a retreat. Everyone scurried to the jeep and they drove away as fast as they could. Until today it is unclear how they got out of there without a scratch.

In the same area near the Lebanese border, there stood a settlement named Kibbutz Manara. The Arab Liberation Army had surrounded Manara and the feeling was that not only was Manara in jeopardy of falling but the nearby settlement at Misgav Am as well. To give you a sense of what the Arab Liberation Army had in mind for us, suffice it say that its symbol was a crooked dagger, dripping blood, piercing a Star of David.

A call went out for volunteers to relieve the siege, and since I was at nearby Kfar Giladi, I was asked to be a part of the group. In our rucksacks we carried ammunition, rifles, grenades, and other supplies. We were planning on carrying out the children on our way out. The road into the kibbutz was completely cut off so our only way in was to climb up the steep mountain terrain. Our guide was a local fellow who presumably knew the way. I say presumably because it soon became evident that we were lost. The only thing to do was to climb all the way down and start over. This time we did so with a new guide and made it up without difficulty.

Manara is today a big tourist attraction with cable cars that give you a spectacular view of the region. But it was a combat zone back then. We began to unload our rucksacks and then went into the dining hall for some food before making our descent. While eating a sandwich, I spotted Jerry Brostoff, who was originally from Leeds but was then a member of Kfar Blum. What alarmed me was that a pin from his grenade, which resembles a key ring, was dangling from his belt. One little tug and we would have all been done for. Everyone except Jerry ran outside as quickly as possible. We then instructed Jerry from outside to slowly remove his belt, take out the pin, and then put it back into the grenade where it rightly belonged. Whatever possessed Jerry to pull a stunt like this I will never know. I don't think he knew either. It may not surprise you to hear that while Jerry did leave Kfar Blum, it was not for a career on the police bomb squad. Instead, he became a prominent professor. What else?

The most dangerous part of our journey turned out to be the incident in the dining hall, though we were, in reality, far from being safe. We still had to make our way down the mountain, this time with children on our backs. I referred earlier to the movie "The Exodus." This scene takes place in the movie and Leon Uris actually travelled to Manara to research the events that I have been speaking about. I met him at the time and thought him to be a real nice chap. Well, if you remember the scene, the children were fast asleep as we had to be very quiet as we passed close to a number of Arab villages. One sound could have alerted the villagers, and then we would have had the Arab

Liberation Army breathing down our necks. Well, you probably will wonder how the children managed to cooperate so completely. They had been drugged by a doctor. It was absolutely necessary and evacuating the children broke with a generally accepted policy which was to leave the children on the kibbutz. It was thought that you will fight much harder when you are defending innocent children. Only under dire circumstances would you evacuate them.

Safed is a beautiful and ancient city. It is a big tourist attraction in the Galilee, famous for its synagogues, and its once thriving artist colony which, much to my disappointment, has declined in recent years. The city had been safely in our hands since May. It had been a very tough battle, made tougher by the fact that the British had handed the police fort over to the Arabs. The Arabs constructed a siege around the Jewish quarter and were hoping to force the city to capitulate. Fortunately, the Palmach was able to break through and send the Arab army into a hasty retreat. There was, however, a fear that they would return. In preparing for a defense of the city, our leadership was concerned that some of the mystical types that composed its inhabitants would not take up arms due to their religious sensibilities. I went down to Safed and joined a group of local kibbutzniks to eyeball the situation. After some reconnaissance activity, it became clear that an attack was highly unlikely and I was allowed to return to the kibbutz.

The police forts that I have jmentioned above were a key to controlling many of the areas. They had been built by the British in 1938, modeled on the police forts that they had built in India during the uprisings there. They were established in Palestine in reaction to the Arab revolts of 1936. It was most unfortunate for us that the British had decided to hand over so many of these forts to the Arabs. We were aided somewhat in that when the British had built these forts they had employed a Jewish contractor. So we had the plans. But we still had to dislodge the Arabs, and since so many of these police forts were built on high ground, that made the job pretty tough. One such place was Nebi Yusha in the Hula Valley. The police fort at Nebi Yusha was

The Founding of Kfar Hanassi

The Police Fort at Nebi Yusha.

positioned on a hilltop. Our forces needed three separate assaults before they were able to capture the fort. On one of the early attempts, men were wounded as they tried to get near the fort. The barrage from the fort was so intense that the rest of the unit had to withdraw temporarily before coming back to retrieve the men. It was too late as the Arabs came out of the safety of the fort and shot dead the wounded soldiers. The third attempt succeeded because they were able to use artillery to pierce the walls of the fort and the Arabs withdrew, but it was quite a price to pay. While I said that those killed were men, I should have qualified that statement. Many were mere boys. If you are in the area, I suggest you visit the cemetery at Nebi Yusha and take a look at the headstones on the graves. You will see that many of the boys were born in the early 1930s. They were 15 and 16 years old, just a few years removed from Bar Mitzvah age. Quite a sobering sight!

Despite there never being an all-out assault on the kibbutz, vigilance was the order of the day. We all stood guard duty and were constantly on the prowl for any unusual enemy movement. An old abandoned hut served as a lookout spot. Once, Mossy Grodsky spotted a Syrian tank and began a full scale alert. We jumped into trenches and were prepared for the worst. After nothing transpired, someone took a pair of binoculars and noticed that the tank was not moving. There was a simple explanation for that; the tank was not a tank. Rather, it was a large black boulder but when seen against the glistening rays of the sun, it was easily mistaken for a tank. While they did not invade, the Syrians did let us know they were in the neighborhood. They intermittently shelled us and though these interruptions were loud and caused some damage, thankfully no casualties were inflicted.

Part of defense, as they say in America, is having a good offense. I took a commando course where I received instruction in blowing up railroad tracks behind enemy lines. It was like something from the exploits of the French Resistance during the war. I learned how to use explosives, inflicting maximum damage to the tracks so that the enemy would not be able to quickly repair them. One of the students was a Yemenite fellow who was rather shocked at all the damage the explosives were going to unleash on the defenseless track. He proposed another solution to achieve the goal of sabotaging the tracks. He told the instructor that all you needed to do was take a wrench and undo the two nuts and bolt that were holding it all together and then carry the railroad ties away without blowing them up. It was all much neater and quieter, or so he claimed. How did he know so much about all this? Apparently, he had pulled this sort of stunt before with some of his buddies and sold the railroad ties off as scrap.

My position within the IDF was nowhere near as exciting as the commando-style course that I have just been describing. I was put in charge of a reserve transport unit. In those days, the unit was composed of civilian trucks. There were fruit trucks, vegetable trucks, and trucks for hauling just about anything you could imagine, several dozen in all. How did I know when we were on alert? There was a prearranged code and I would receive a call in the middle of the night

I drove many different kinds of trucks during my years on the kibbutz. In this case, I am perched up against a White truck, which is a reference to the manufacturer and not the color of the truck.

and be told to bring the unit to such and such a point at 6:00 A.M. In those days despite the security around the kibbutzim, no one locked the doors to their individual abodes. I would travel to the neighboring kibbutzim and knowing where all the individuals in the unit slept, would awaken them from their slumber and tell them to meet me at the rendezvous point. They may have objected a bit as most sensible people do when you rouse them in the middle of the night, but they would show up. That was the thing about Israel. People complained plenty, but, when push came to shove, they did their jobs.

In addition to serving in a transportation unit, I had been doing a lot of driving for the kibbutz. Once I was behind the wheel of a Mack truck to Haifa to pick up a load of feed and grain. It was sometime in the spring of 1949 and there were no modern highways back then. The road consisted of rough and unpaved cobblestones. It was single lanes all the way and there was a pull-off every couple of miles to allow a vehicle to pass. Pulling into the Haifa port, my truck and I along with it were commandeered by the army. What was the reason for this hasty action? Operation Uvda was underway, led by one of our top commanders, General Yigael Yadin, who would later become a political figure and prominent archeologist. General Yadin had managed to capture Eilat. He was, however, in desperate need of supplies.

We left Haifa in a large convoy. There were many others like myself who had also been commandeered. Unlike the convoy trip from Jerusalem, the main danger was not from hostile Arabs but rather from the road itself. While the road was fine all the way down to Beersheba, it began to deteriorate until there was no road at all, just tracks in the sand to guide you through the Negev. I was given a second driver to help me navigate but just before we came to a spot called Maale Akrabim (Scorpions Pass), the man was ordered to get out of the truck. Apparently, they were worried that given the steepness of the pass, the truck may not make it. This way, they reasoned, they would lose only one driver rather than two. It was a bit unsettling when you stared out the window and saw the area littered with the skeletons of vehicles that did not make it. They were fair warning of what could happen if you were not real careful and my truck was carrying twenty tons of supplies to boot. Fortunately, I made it.

We arrived in Eilat and unloaded the trucks. Though Eilat is today a thoroughly modern city, with a busy port and first class hotels, it amounted to little more than a few small huts in 1949. In addition to being hungry, thirsty, and a little tired, I was anxious to get back to the kibbutz for Shabbat dinner as it was already Thursday afternoon. The other drivers also wanted to get back to their homes. The army had other ideas. They wanted us to wait around and drive another convoy but did not know when we would leave. We waited for a while. An officer finally came out and told us that he could not keep us in Eilat indefinitely, but if we wanted to go back to our homes, we were on our own. Of course, we were in the middle of a war, but I was able to get back in time.

The war would end with a series of armistice agreements signed with the Arabs during 1949. The death toll was high; 6,300 Jews died, including both civilians and soldiers. Some of those who perished were experienced men and some were boys like those at Nebi Yusha. Some were sabras who had been trained by the Night Squadrons set up by the legendary British officer and hero to the state of Israel, Orde Wingate. Others had been green Holocaust survivors, who had been handed a rifle soon after they landed in the country. Others were civilians, old women, young children, caught in the crossfire or murdered deliberately by Arabs. Many more than the 6,300 killed had been wounded and many more would suffer similar fates in the wars and terrorist attacks that lay ahead.

We had survived. Now we had to build the kibbutz. One of the biggest obstacles we faced was the land itself. Israel is a land flowing with milk and honey as I first heard in cheder. Mansura, however, seemed to be overflowing with boulders and large rocks. I was told that these were left over from the volcanic eruptions that helped create the Jordan River. Whatever its causes, the reality was they were so

On the rocky grounds of Mansura with Ossy Edelstein
and unidentified friend on the right.

deeply embedded that every time you thought you had actually gotten down to the soil, you would discover a whole new layer of rocks. You would be clearing the same piece of earth four and five times over.

How did we clear the land? We used a rooter that was pulled by one of those big D8 tractors. The rooter's three deep prongs would break up the earth so we could remove the large stones and boulders. We would then put these heavy rocks onto a sledge and have them pulled by a smaller tractor which we then placed at the edge of the field. If you go to the kibbutz today, you will still see them resting there. The whole process took months to complete and was extremely grueling.

With the land cleared, it was time to plant crops. There were corn, wheat, and vegetables. There were plum, peach, and apple orchards. For livestock, the Jewish Agency provided us with ten cows for the dairy and chickens for the chicken house. Though we were growing food, we did not necessarily have a lot to eat. We had not yet constructed the dining hall so we used a hastily constructed wooden hut in which to eat our meals. Due to its rather unstable construction, it reminded me of a Sukkah like the one I had climbed up to fetch the apple in the West Ham Synagogue. As sometimes happens when you sit in a Sukkah, we were besieged with bees or even worse, hornets. Initially, our breakfast rations consisted of two pieces of bread. What did we put on it? We received from America a rather foul-smelling fish paste. But I was so hungry from all the work that it tasted like a fine marmalade jam.

CHAPTER EIGHT

Kibbutz Life

It is the 100th year of the kibbutz movement so it seems apropos that I should be writing about kibbutz life now. You may be wondering how the kibbutz is run. Who makes the decisions? The kibbutz is an exercise in pure democracy, with the kibbutz membership voting in general meetings that are held weekly. There are committees which deal with every aspect of kibbutz life. One of the most important of these committees is the works committee, which determines what job kibbutz members will perform. Some people had regular jobs. Others received daily assignments to accommodate wherever extra labor was needed.

I was fortunate to have a regular job. As we accumulated a fair amount of machinery, we needed someone to repair and maintain that equipment. It was decided that that person should be me. I was sent to an established kibbutz to work in their garage before taking over in ours. The kibbutz turned out to be Kfar Giladi, which was founded when World War One was still raging. It was originally a sister settlement of Tel Chai, the settlement that was immortalized by the heroism of Joseph Trumpeldor, and was an inspiration to Zionists everywhere. You could feel its rich history in the night air. That history was shaped by many battles and a war which had just recently ended. The kibbutz was near the Lebanese border, and if you travel there today, you will see a memorial to the many skirmishes that took place on the kibbutz.

I had been known as Alfy Nathan throughout my time in Israel. But I started to call myself Avraham Natan during my time at Giladi. This was because most of the members there were not English speakers so I decided to Hebraize my name as so many others had done. Of course, when people would come to visit they would always asked for Alfy. People on the kibbutz did not know who Alfy was. Eventually they realized that Avraham was Alfy. So once they found out my English name, everyone started calling me Alfy. I guess what I said at the beginning of this book really rang true—everyone calls me Alfy.

In the kibbutz, I lived in a tiny room, even smaller than my pineapple box enclosure in the French villa. It was directly above the dining room, which was a very active place. It was there that I met one of the few English speakers on Kfar Giladi. His name was Shlomo (Sonny) Weintraub, an American who worked in the dining room. Originally from Baltimore, he had served in the Machal (foreign volunteers) during illegal immigration and the War of Independence and suffered a head wound in the fighting by the Syrian/Lebanese border.

Sonny became romantically involved with a certain young lady on the kibbutz who was anxious to become Mrs. Sonny Weintraub. He was less than anxious for such a development. This girl was a very determined young lady and she kept the pressure on him. When he continued to hold out, her mother came to pay him a visit to provide some encouragement. Again, Sonny declined. The mother became furious and decided that if Sonny would not marry her daughter, he was not going to marry anyone. An argument ensued in the dining room and she brandished a dangerous weapon, an old-fashioned rolling pin, and began chasing him. Well, fortunately, Sonny could still run and run he did all the way out of the kibbutz. For someone who had been on a crew that had played cat and mouse with the British navy, this surely was his finest escape. As a postscript, I should add that the story has a happy ending because he ended up marrying a lovely woman, who presumably had a friendlier mother than his former girlfriend from Kfar Giladi. He found success as an artist; one of his paintings hangs in my home.

It was not all hard work in the early years. Here I am
hiking near the Lebanese border.

The original size of our group at Kfar Hanassi was forty strong,
which included some children. Our numbers would increase over the
years. Though our roots were in Habonim and the Farm, as we grew,
we started to add new members who were not connected with either.
People were always passing through. Some would stay for a short time.
Some would stay for a longer time. And some would become members. Sometimes fate intervened. David Levy, who was from Manchester, came ostensibly to give regards to Gershon Epstein, a member who
was also from Manchester. He arrived during the day sometime and,
after seeing Gershon, had planned to continue his tour of Israel. Well,
at 5:30, he got ready to leave and was surprised to learn that the last

bus of the day had already gone. So he stayed another day and then another and another and so on until he realized that he loved the kibbutz. He became a member, married a girl from the kibbutz, and had three children before passing away.

Many married couples grew out of the core group. There were reasons for that. First of all, we shared much in common and were ideologically and culturally suited for one another. We had become friends during our stay on the Farm and on the kibbutz. And of course, the kibbutz was close quarters, and, due to our isolated life, meeting people from outside the kibbutz was difficult. When the second generation came around this would change dramatically. I met my wife, Louie, on the kibbutz. I had heard of her but did not know her when I was in England. Despite our mutual involvement in Habonim, our backgrounds were really quite different. While my family was Eastern European, Louie's family were Dutch Jews who had immigrated to England. While my family was very traditionally oriented in respect to religion, Louie's was fairly secular. Our interests were vastly different as well. While Louie was a tremendously creative person, a gifted artist and singer, I was, as you may have noticed, interested in mechanical and practical matters. Nevertheless, we fell very much in love. She loved and was completely devoted to the kibbutz. Her sister, Debbie, with whom she was very close, was also a founding member. Debbie had married Shmuel Khatzor, one of our most influential members and a force in the kibbutz's leadership.

We were married in Rosh Pina under a chupah (canopy) outside of the rabbi's home. It was quite a sight as the sounds of chickens clucking about were interspersed with the sounds of the glass breaking and the traditional shouts of "Mazel Tov!" There was a simple wedding meal, and then afterward, everyone went right back to work. As we were all very informal, kibbutz weddings generally meant that the groom would don a white shirt and a pair of jeans. The brides, however even when they were strong kibbutzniks, occasionally wore a long gown, if they could get one.

Some weddings were held in the kibbutz's amphitheater, which was really beautiful. There is an interesting story behind its construction. I think it was the Australian Zionist Federation, which had taken a good deal of interest in us, and had donated money for us to build an amphitheater. As our needs were always pressing, we must have used the money for something else. One day we received word that someone from its organization was coming to the kibbutz to see the amphitheater. He would arrive in two days. We were in a mild panic. We got to work in a hurry. By the next day, tractors came and leveled out the land, digging out the earth for the amphitheater. We then put in concrete seating. In twenty four hours it was all done.

The same group decided, upon seeing our conditions, to donate money so that we could build a swimming pool. As this was still the 1950s, swimming pools were quite rare in Israel. Accepting the money created quite a controversy. I, for one, was firmly against it. I felt that there were more important needs in Israel at the time than a swimming pool for Kfar Hannasi. The money would have been better spent on providing basic services to one of the many development towns that had sprung up to accommodate the mass influx of immigrants. My view was in the minority. Someone far more influential than Alfy Nathan stated that the Australians could see that we were living in difficult conditions right on the border. We were assuming great risk in taking on part of the security burden. If it made the Aussies feel better for us to have a swimming pool then who were we to refuse them this pleasure? I felt that this was sheer and utter nonsense. I pointed out that we lived on the border because we wanted to, not because we had to. As you can rightly guess, I lost the debate and we got a swimming pool.

One group who benefited from the pool, even though they never swam in it, were our Bedouin neighbors in Tuba. Our relationship with the village was cordial though sometimes issues sprang up that needed to be discussed. It was uncanny how they managed to show up just as our kibbutz women managed to be out in their bathing suits sunbathing; just like clockwork.

One of the issues that often reared itself was theft. Even though we had a fence around the buildings of the kibbutz, things would invariably turn up missing. There was no doubt as to the ethnicity of the culprits, but you did not want to accuse the whole village. Sometimes the police force in Rosh Pina would bring back an item that was taken from the kibbutz and had been found by them in the course of their work. Sometimes it was found in Tuba. Occasionally, we did not even realize that the item was missing. Stealing was our biggest worry. We could travel and hitchhike the area without ever being concerned about being attacked or ambushed by our neighbors.

In the early 1950s, a major priority of the government was the draining of the Hula. This, naturally enough, solved the problem of malaria. The company which spearheaded the huge undertaking was a Jewish-owned firm out of Chicago. They made a series of canals, and used pontoon boats in what was a fascinating job to watch. While working on the project, an underground spring was found that emitted something like 48,000 gallons of water per minute, a tremendous source of fresh water. They dug a hole in the mountain and put three pumps in. The reason it was put in the side of a mountain was that in the event of an air attack, our water source would be protected. A six inch line was eventually put in and came straight to the kibbutz. No more tanker trips to Rosh Pina. Of course, our Bedouin neighbors did not share our good fortune though the line passed near Tuba.

It was not unusual to see our neighbors going down to the local spring to bring back water. It was quite a sight as a man would be riding on his donkey with his wife or wives trailing behind. The women would carry the jug down. After filling it up, they would carry it back on top of their head. Not too chivalrous perhaps, but this was how they had been doing it for thousands of years. They were in for a change.

We felt that the right thing to do would be to run a line that was connected to our lines all the way into Tuba. We thought we were doing a good deed, but not long afterward, Tuba residents came to us to complain. What was the problem? Apparently, the village chief was charging a fee for every jerry can of water that the residents took. He saw the line as his and it became a moneymaker. It was surely an unintended consequence, but now we had to decide what to do. Our solution was to tell the Mukhtar (chief) that he could keep the line for himself. We would run a second line for the people.

From the Mukhtar's point of view, the water line had also been a way for him to assume some power. Ever since the village had come under Israeli rule, he had lost a good deal of power. His villagers now voted in Israeli elections. They were learning to read and write. There was a municipal police force in Rosh Pina that enforced the laws of the state. People were not only freer, they were becoming wealthier. Many set up small businesses, particularly in the building trades. They became active building not only roads, but homes as well. If you go to the village today, you will see satellite dishes on some of their homes in Tuba. And these are big, beautiful homes. They would never live so well in Lebanon, Syria or even Jordan. Certainly not under Palestinian rule, which most are not very keen on, or such was always my impression. I have to admit that when I visited recently, I did see a Palestinian flag flying on one of the homes, which is an unusual sight, but troublesome nonetheless.

An illustration of the newfound prosperity of the village could be seen on a visit several years ago. I was out walking with Lil, when one of my old friends from the village happened to spot me and picked us up. He was driving a nice truck, in this case, with the name of his business written in Arabic on the side. He seemed glad to see me and, after a warm greeting, we started to speak of the old days. I asked him how things were going, and how his business was? Very well, he told me. I asked him how his wives were doing and he told me that he had recently gotten a new one from Syria. With a wink and a nod, he told me she was a redhead.

If our Bedouin neighbors were a little shocked at the swimming attire of our female members, they would have been positively mystified to hear that on the kibbutz, women enjoyed complete equality. The kibbutz did not need a women's liberation movement. We were living it. Women had fought alongside men during the War of Independence and continued to perform tasks in the state that had been historically associated with males. I should add that among all of our many accomplishments in Israel, I believe that we were one of the first nations to have a female prime minister. In our case, it was Golda Meir.

Perhaps the most controversial aspect of kibbutz life was the way children were raised. Though this would change over time, both of my daughters grew up in the children's houses. Problems were created when the babies were very young and mothers would have to go to the nursery to feed them. As the children became toddlers though, it was clear there were many advantages to this system. Although many people thought there was a strong ideological basis for the children's houses, the primary reason was that it allowed mothers to work during the day rather than having to focus on caring for the children. It was a question of division of labor, although I must say that those kibbutz members responsible for the children's care were primarily women.

We spent time with our children in the evening for several hours after dinner. This is what people today would call "quality time." Without the stress and strain of having to care for the children all day long, you really got to enjoy them, playing with them and listening to what they had learned that day in school. I still remember the wonderful evening walks I took with my daughters, Rena and Yael. One unique aspect of kibbutz life was having all sorts of animals around and I don't mean dogs and cats. Of course, the children enjoyed it greatly. I would take the girls down on Shabbat afternoon and they would pet the animals. No need to go to a petting zoo. Not just then, but during the week they could view a whole world that some children only learn about in textbooks. They saw horses grazing and running, cows being milked, calves being born, sheep being sheared, and chickens doing whatever it is that chickens do. It was a unique childhood for them and I still remember the expressions in their eyes and the smiles on their faces whenever they viewed these wonderful events.

There was another unique aspect to having the children's houses. I have heard from my own daughters that the relationship that they developed with those of their age in the children's house was very special. In a sense, they established a closeness that even transcended what one would feel toward a brother or sister. Even when they are out of touch for periods of time, they seem to be able to pick up where they left off with those they had grown up with in the children's house. When they need help of some kind, say in an emergency, they can count on each other. It is a unique system, though in the end, the traditional family dynamics would win out. Perhaps that is the way it should be. Perhaps not.

We had started the kibbutz with just a few children, but as more and more of us married and had families, we needed to educate the children. Initially, the children travelled to one of the larger kibbutzim and enrolled in their school. There arose a strong desire for us to start our own school. Unfortunately, there were not enough children to make this feasible. We needed more children and travelled to Jerusalem to inquire about the possibility of adopting some. There was no shortage of orphans or those from troubled homes in those years. So we adopted 10 or 15 youngsters and they helped form the nucleus of our first class. These children all did rather well. Some even stayed on the kibbutz, becoming members and having families of their own.

Having a school was important. There were other services, however, to which we needed to have access. One such service was medical care. At the beginning, we had a doctor come to us from Rosh Pina. He lived there in a beautiful stone house surrounded by old, cobblestone roads. He would come to the kibbutz on horseback once a week. Talk about a house call. Eventually, we got a doctor who was a paid member of the kibbutz. He would visit the neighboring kibbutzim in addition to taking care of us. We also had a nurse, Irit Ben Chaim, who had fallen in love and married a Habonim friend of mine, Moshe Ben Chaim (Moshe Tober).

Children on the kibbutz were born in hospitals. I still remember when my older daughter, Rena, was born. It was 1950 and Louie gave birth in the Scottish hospital in Tiberias. A kibbutz girl, our daughter, a Sabra, born in a hospital started by Protestant missionaries in the 19th century. Quite something! What a glorious sight to be sitting there, a new father holding his newborn daughter. On a kibbutz, the birth of a child symbolizes something more than the great personal joy that every parent surely feels. A child symbolizes the increased strength of the kibbutz and the growing population of a young country.

Yael was born five years later. She came into this world in the city of Safed, in a government hospital. It was every bit as powerful and exciting looking into her eyes as when her older sister was born. How did we get the women to the hospital to give birth? Of course, no one owned a car because no one owned anything, but we will get into that soon enough. The kibbutz did own a car. Members had rotating driver duty. If it was your turn, you were essentially on call until the following morning. If someone needed to be picked up in Rosh Pina, you would go. If someone had an emergency, you would take him wherever he needed to go. Most importantly, if a woman went into labor, you had to be prepared to drive pretty quickly. Later, we acquired an old ambulance from Magen David Adom, the Israeli version of the Red Cross. We relied on each other to handle every situation that would emerge. We did not phone 911. We were 911.

While entertainment may not be as essential as education or medical care, it was an integral part of our lives. We were just like everyone else and needed a break from the rigors of kibbutz life. Though people might go to Rosh Pina or Safed for a motion picture or to sip coffee in a café today, those were unimaginable diversions in my day. Our entertainment was strictly home grown. Once a week we would show a movie in our makeshift cinema. What did our makeshift cinema consist of? Our silver screen was a large white bed sheet that hung outside the dining hall. Though it was not quite the Theatre Royale in Stratford, it did the job rather nicely.

The best entertainment was reserved for the zigs (skits) that were performed with some regularity. It was a night to which everyone looked forward. Again, we did not need to bring in any comedians or actors, not that we could have. We had ample talent in our midst. Our funniest member was surely Mossy Grodsky. He was our Jackie Mason, or perhaps more appropriately given that he was English, our Bud Flanagan. (Flanagan was a prominent British comedian of my youth who used to perform at the Palladium in London together with a group known as "the Crazy Gang." Bud Flanagan's real name was Chaim Reuven Weintrop.) To me, Mossy was just as talented as Flanagan. He had a great ear for accents, and was a superb mimic. He was behind putting together all of the fabulous shows which I think compare favorably with what you would see today in a comedy club.

Mossy was an interesting bloke. He was not from the East End but rather he hailed from Northwest London, working as a hairdresser before he came to Israel. If opposites really do attract, the proof was Mossy and his wife. She had, like a fair number of kibbutz people, come over on Kindertransport and was a fairly reserved, quiet type. Of course, Mossy was a raconteur of the first order and never at a loss for words. Most of all, he was a master of finding the humor in the most mundane areas of kibbutz life.

Shalom Namally was another member of the comedy team. He was also from London but had been placed in Norwood Jewish Orphanage when he was young. He had two older brothers who had already settled in Palestine when I was still training on the Farm. One day one of his brothers came back to England to visit him in the orphanage and decided that this was no place for a budding Zionist. They just walked out with him straight away and took him to stay with us on the Farm.

While these special occasions were wonderful, perhaps the greatest moments of life on the kibbutz could be found in the simple day-to-day interactions with fellow members. Dinnertime stands out. Not for the food of course, but for the fact that it was a communal dinner. In America, it is not uncommon for people to eat in front of a television, or read a newspaper while dining. There are families where individuals eat at different times. On the kibbutz such isolation would be impossible. Dinner was to mix with other people.

The most special dinner of the week was of course, Friday night. Though many of us had veered a bit from some of the Jewish traditions that we were raised with, Shabbat dinner was still Shabbat dinner. After we concluded eating our festive meal, the evening would continue with Israeli dancing. There were many different types of dances that would be heartily enjoyed on Friday evenings. Most are familiar with the Hora, a dance with origins in Eastern Europe that became a real mainstay of Israel folk life. Since Israel received immigrants from so many different places, people brought their dances with them, just as they had brought their food. Many caught on with the kibbutzim. My favorites were the fantastic Yemenite dances. They required great synchronization what with all the hopping and pivoting. I suppose they are roughly akin to today's line dancing but with much more feeling and passion.

If the chalutz spirit was on display for Shabbat dinner, it was even more evident for the holidays. There was an abundance of what we called ruach (spirit). The best holidays were those whose message was easily adapted to the kibbutz life. Passover was a highlight. We were all raised with the traditional Seder and Haggadah. While much of the Seder remained in tact, we made some contemporary changes that reflected our own struggles with freedom. We clearly identified strongly with the Exodus story. Just as the Hebrews had been in bondage to Pharoah, we had been in a sort of bondage while living in the Galut (exile). Just as God had emancipated the Hebrews and Moses had led them out to Israel, Zionism and Habonim had done pretty much the same for us. The similarities extended to modern times too. If you were not a stickler for historical accuracy you could make the case that just as our enemies in biblical times were Egypt and Pharoah, ours in the 50s and 60s were Egypt and Nasser.

Other holidays like Sukkot and Shavout took on a decidedly unique flavor, with an emphasis on their agricultural and naturalistic elements. Some holidays were obvious expressions of our own sense of nationalism like Hanukkah. Others went well with our sense of joy like Purim. Still others, like Tu Beshvat (the birthday for trees), took on a significance far greater than it ever had before in Jewish history. There were Israeli holidays like Independence Day to celebrate but every holiday was made more meaningful by living in Israel. This was, after all, where it all happened.

One of the daily pleasures on the kibbutz was taking a shower at the end of a workday. We had progressed past manually pouring the water through the old cucumber cans. We now had real showers but these were communal showers. Since we were still living in wooden huts, private showers were out of the question. Communal showers meant that you got the opportunity to joke around with one another; laughing and singing could be heard from a good distance away. The men's and women's showers were separated by a corrugated wall. You could hear the ladies going through the same routine as us and friendly banter would go back and forth.

When we built more modern housing and when we were able to afford it, we would eventually install showers in the homes. Not that they were up to the level of the American showers of today but they spelled the end of the communal showers. It was not that most of us did not appreciate the added comforts that having a private shower signified. I have heard people say that when we did away with the communal showers, it came with a price. The price was a steep one; a decline in the communal life of the kibbutz. It may seem like a small thing but I think it was significant.

The evolution of having telephones on the kibbutz is a perfect example of how progress and technology also have a price. In all of my years there, we never had phones in the homes. The phone was in the office. When there was a call for you, and there were precious few as it was very expensive, someone would run around and fetch you. You were totally dependent on one another. Secrets were naturally hard to keep on the kibbutz, and there was not a lot of privacy, but that was part of its appeal. I remember when the kibbutz got telephones. It was well after I left and I was visiting with Lil. We were sitting around with two other couples when one of them left to go home. They lived practically next door and they called to say they arrived home safely and continued speaking as if they were still sitting with us. They were so enamored of the novelty of it all. Who could rightly blame them when much of the country had already received one?

One of the big issues revolved around private property. Technically, there was not supposed to be any. We lived in fairly spartan conditions at the beginning and things slowly got a little better. The furniture was limited and plain and there was not much to buy even if you had the money with which to buy it. Most people in Israel had very little. When you received an outside gift, you were supposed to hand it in to the kibbutz. Louie was a stickler for this. I give her great credit because she had tremendous integrity when it came to things like that. I, on the other hand, did not think it was all that big of a deal. Once when Barry and Lottie were visiting, they brought us a box of tea, which was considered an expensive gift at the time. I am sure it was good tea, but we never found out. It went straight into the coffers of the kibbutz.

One of the major advantages to not owning anything was that it was supposed to limit certain very negative emotions like jealousy and envy. You could not be envious at the size of someone else's bank account for no one had a bank account, at least he was not supposed to have one. In America, there is an expression, "keeping up with the Joneses." I am fortunate today to live in a very fine home in a very nice suburb of Chicago. There are many homes larger and fancier than mine. It does not bother me in the slightest, but there are people who find that they are not able to enjoy what they have because others have more. It is a sad reality of living in a capitalistic and materialistic world. Communal living and sharing were supposed to mean an end to envy. As we shall see soon enough though, the dreams and hopes of a socialist paradise are difficult to realize.

Kibbutz Life

This shunning of things material surely was one of the reasons that people throughout the world took an interest in kibbutz in the 1950s but especially in the 1960s. We had many young people coming through the kibbutz. Some had been sent by their parents because they had a drug problem or were engaging in some form of rebellious behavior. Some were actually looking for a more meaningful life. Kibbutz was a natural place to look. They may have stayed a week, a month or endured a full six-month term as a volunteer. A small minority would desire to become members. We accepted nearly everybody. There were only a few types we avoided. If they were using drugs while on the kibbutz, that was a problem. If they had a propensity for stealing, that was not good either. But what you really had to watch out for though were lazy people, those who saw in the kibbutz a way of opting out of the pressures that came with having to earn a living. I should add that those who came to find out what kibbutz was all about were not necessarily Jewish. There were plenty of European and American Gentiles, attracted more by communitarianism than Zionism.

One young person who came to the kibbutz for extended visits was my nephew, Lawrence Nathan, Sid's son. He did not come because he was disenchanted with his life; far from it. He would become a very successful doctor. He was active in Habonim in London and clearly had strong feelings about Israel. He may have been influenced by stories he heard about me or from me when he was growing up. He came a number of times visiting or volunteering on the kibbutz. I think he enjoyed it and I know I enjoyed spending time with him.

While my brand of Zionism may have influenced Lawrence, the person who probably most came under my spell was my brother Barry. When I last spoke of him, he was a child trying to make it through the war. Like me, his formal schooling ended while in his teenage years. He began to work for Sid, who had opened up an appliance store in London. Like me, Barry was mechanically inclined. And he spent time on one of the Hachsharot farms in England. He had learned a lot of the same skills that I had a decade earlier, important things like how to plow a field and how to milk a cow. Perhaps the best thing that happened to him in joining Habonim is that it served as a catalyst for meeting his future wife, Lottie, who had come over on Kindertransport and had lost her whole family in the Holocaust.

I got the word by mail that Barry was coming together with his group to settle in Israel, just as I had come five years earlier. I met them in the Haifa port in October of 1952. His group went to a place called Gal Ed, close to Haifa, for one year just as we had spent time in Kfar Blum and Hadera. The early fifties was a difficult period economically. There was a great deal of scarcity, and though Barry had been through the rationing during the war, this may have taken him a bit by surprise. I remember him telling me that he was getting one egg a week and the big treat was fried cauliflower. His group relocated to Kibbutz Amiad. He and Lottie would remain there for five years.

I think Barry became somewhat disenchanted with certain aspects of kibbutz life and he moved to town. He took a job operating a bulldozer and would travel the country, taking on jobs wherever they were available. Whenever he had a job near the kibbutz, he would stay with us. He then went to work for an American company, Miles Laboratories of Elkhart, Indiana, working his way up the ladder of its Israeli subsidiary. His family spent some of the holidays with us during those years and we all enjoyed it.

Barry was not my only sibling to be in Israel during the decade of the 50s. My sister Sally and her husband, Henry Ebner, came in the late 40s from England. He was a very interesting fellow. Originally from Poland, he had come to France and joined the French army. During the war he was captured by the Germans. He managed to escape and made his way to Algiers, where he saw action again and was seriously wounded. He was taken to England to recover, and that is how he met my sister. Well, Henry was anxious to get to Israel and, after being married in Paris, the two of them settled in Jaffa in an old Arab house where the kitchen was actually outside, sheltered only by a sheet-metal roof. Henry was a great lover of Tanach (Hebrew Bible) and was very handy so it is safe to say that he fit in well with the family. He started a plating company but ran into a serious problem. He was unable to buy the metals he needed for the business because of the general problem with importing goods at the time. (We lacked hard currency in those days.) In the fifties they moved to Montreal and found success building log cabins in the Quebec countryside which people used as summer homes.

One of the greatest challenges that any immigrant faces is learning a new language. Though I had learned Hebrew as part of my religious studies as a youth, modern Hebrew was something with which I had only a limited familiarity. Sure, I had picked up a few expressions on the Farm, but when you are around other English speakers, there is always the temptation to speak only English. Kfar Hanassi was dominated by Anglo speakers and most of us continued with our mother tongue, interspersed with a smattering of Hebrew expressions and phrases. There were several families who resolved to speak only Hebrew but they were in the minority. Of course, we still needed to be able to communicate in Hebrew when we left the confines of the kibbutz. I was able to communicate adequately and learned the language, struggling with the Israeli newspapers. My dictionary rarely left my side. I never felt completely comfortable in speaking Hebrew. My dikduk (grammar) was far from perfect. If you have visited Israel, you may have observed that native born Israelis are not shy about correcting you. The difference was noticeable when I was around my brother Barry. He spoke a fluent Hebrew with perfect grammar and could have been mistaken for a Sabra.

Young people and committed Zionists were not the only parties interested in seeing what kibbutzim were all about. Since many settlements were major innovators in farming methods, we attracted a variety of agronomists and agriculturalists. I don't know if we were all so smart, but as they say "necessity is the mother of invention" and necessity was constantly forcing us to come up with interesting solutions to problems that we faced, whether in the cotton fields or the chicken coops.

One day I received a call from an official in our government that Great Britain's Minister of Agriculture was visiting Israel and wanted to see the kibbutz. Would I take him around? Certainly I would. He was a very pleasant chap and seemed noticeably impressed by what he saw. He was staying overnight and there were no hotels in the area and the kibbutz did not yet have a guest house. Where did we put people up? We would put guests in the homes of kibbutz members who were traveling.

The minister seemed to get a restful night's sleep when I saw him the following morning at breakfast. In between bites of his omelet he asked me in whose home he had slept in the previous evening? I told him that he had slept in the bed of the kibbutz's shepherd. He seemed totally mystified. "Alfy, what kind of a shepherd studies Greek philosophy?" I told him that Lenny was a great lover of Aristotle, Socrates, and Plato. The minister just could not believe it. He had met shepherds throughout England. Greek philosophy was not a major avocation among this set.

This all points to something rather interesting. Despite the fact that much of the work that we were doing was physical, many of our members were cultured, well-read, and intellectually curious. You could find them reading and engaging in spirited discussions about a whole range of topics. We had an active choir and our most literate members published an interesting newsletter. Had they not decided to go to Israel and join the kibbutz, many of our members would have become scientists, engineers, artists, and teachers. They chose kibbutz because they wanted to build up the country. They were willing to sacrifice. It shows you the tremendous allure of idealism.

The kibbutz movement together with the moshavim represented the elite of the country. (While the word *moshav* sometimes connotes a settlement, here we speak of cooperative farming. While there are two types of moshavim, one of which is closer to a kibbutz, the basic difference between moshav and kibbutz is that the moshav allows for private property and sometimes even private profits.) The senior officers of the army together with the leadership of the government mostly came from one or the other. This was especially true during the first two decades of the state. Since we were on the border, we were part of the security apparatus of the country. It gave us a high status and provided us with access to many senior leaders.

While I would not want to be accused of excessive name dropping, I would be remiss if I did not share my impressions of some of the leaders of that era. When I spoke earlier of the chalutz (pioneer) spirit and the toughness that it took to hold out against the many enemies of Israel, a man who comes to mind was General Rafael Eitan. Eitan had served in the Palmach and then once the state was formed was one of the early paratrooper commanders, ultimately rising to chief of staff of the army. He fought in every war and in 1973, led the counterattack in the north when the Syrians threatened not only to take the Golan Heights back but penetrate into the Galilee. Rafi, as they called him, represented that can-do spirit of 1948, a man totally connected to the land. A secular nationalist, he made the security of the state his personal mission. He died several years ago and with him went a world and a spirit that we are unlikely to see again.

I got the opportunity to meet another great military persona in Moshe Dayan. He was truly a larger-than-life figure. While America may have had its MacArthur and Patton, Israel had Moshe Dayan. He was the bravest in battle and had a razor-sharp mind that was always running fast and furious. He had interests well beyond the military and politics and was considered something of an amateur archeologist. There were plenty of rumors about some of Dayan's less than stellar personal qualities, but on the few times when I was in his company, I thoroughly enjoyed him. He was charming and urbane, true enough. I also found him to be a nice and friendly person who seemed genuinely interested in what you had to say. This cannot be said of all our leaders. It is true that he was demanding and would ask tough questions, but every time I was in his company was memorable. I just had tremendous respect for the man.

Moshe Dayan on the battlefield.

One time I was visiting him at his home and we went walking together in his beautiful garden. What made the garden so special was that there were various pieces of antiquities scattered throughout the greenery. He had acquired this fantastic collection by taking

David Ben-Gurion was the man who had asked us to
come and settle in Mansura. Here he comes to
see how things are going.
L to R: me, Bernie Marks, Shuki Cohen, Ben-Gurion, Michael Cohen.

pieces before the authorities or the government archeologists arrived
on the scene of newly discovered digs. It was a bit controversial to say
the least. As we were speaking, Dayan was approached by one of his
lieutenants whose rank far exceeded that of a lieutenant. He pointed
to one of the pieces and said, "Don't show these to Alfy. He's a kibbutznik." I promised not to turn him in and we all got a good laugh.

I should really have begun this discussion with the man who had sent us to Kfar Hanassi, David Ben-Gurion. Though he resembled a mild mannered professor, with his diminutive stature and unkept, flowing white mane, he was full of fire and steely resolve. He took a great interest in all of the kibbutzim and had great confidence in us. We never wanted to let him down. Though he is associated with Sde Boker in the Negev where he spent his latter years, he was a frequent visitor to the Galilee. Tiberias was a favorite of his and he would relax in a hotel that was on Lake Kineret.

We would travel from the kibbutz to visit him. His wife Paula, who was born in Europe but raised in the United States, kept a watchful eye on him. Ben-Gurion was afraid of no one with the possible exception of his wife. I can't blame him on that score. She was a pretty fierce lady. Short of a national emergency, she would not awaken him from his midday nap. If you wanted to speak with him, you would simply have to wait for him to get up. It was worth the wait.

Chaim Weizmann figures prominently in this book. He inspired me in my youth. We named the kibbutz for him. I got the opportunity to meet him on several occasions in his home in Rehovot. Despite his busy schedule, and he was president of both Israel and of the scientific institute that he had founded, he still made time to see people. His wife would host afternoon tea and a bunch of us would go. She was quite a lady in her own right, a very accomplished physician and as devoted to the fledgling country as her husband. So there was little old Alfy and his friends, simple Jewish boys from Habonim, sipping tea with the Weizmanns. Quite something!

Ezer Weizman, Chaim Weizmann's nephew was another unique figure. He was very determined to be his own man, even changing the spelling of his last name to differentiate himself from his famous uncle. Serving in the RAF during the war, he would become the founder and head of the Israeli Air Force. He could fly any plane imaginable and often did. His knowledge of aviation was stunning. Though his uncle had made his mark as a scientist and a diplomat, Ezer was not naturally disposed to diplomacy. Though he would also serve as president of Israel, his lack of tact frequently landed him in hot water. He persisted in speaking his mind and it was a brilliant mind at that. Our air force was one of the reasons we were victorious in the Six Day War and it was Weizman who led the surprise raids on the Egyptian air fields that decimated their air force.

If you bear with me, I want to go back to my friend, the British Minister of Agriculture. I escorted the minister to a Friday night dinner held at the home of Moshe Dayan. The Weizmans were there as well. (Moshe Dayan's wife, Ruth whom he later divorced, and Ezer Weizman's wife, Reuma, were sisters.) When I was introduced to Mrs. Weizman, she greeted me warmly, "Alfy how have you been? I have not seen you in so many years!" Of course, I had not seen her in many years either. We were old friends. I knew her as a Ruchama Schwartz, a young woman who spent some time in England working for the Jewish Agency during the years when I was on the Farm. We became good friends and it was quite an unusual place for a reunion, Friday night dinner at the Dayans. I should also add that although Moshe Dayan was known for being very secular, there was no question that it was Shabbat that night. Sabbath candles were burning with all their radiant splendor.

Speaking of England, I had not been back to my country of birth since I made the secret trip on behalf of the organization in 1947. I was after a map of the North Sea at the time, and if you remember, I had assumed the identity of an officer of a Canadian freighter that had been docked in Marseilles. It was now 1956 and in planning a trip to England, I did not have anything clandestine in mind. I simply wanted to visit family and thought it might be interesting to travel as Alfy Nathan for a change.

There was one problem with this plan. I had given up my passport to the organization when I began working for it, making my way to Israel on the forged Canadian one. Now I needed my British passport back. I was told to go to such-and-such a street in Tel Aviv and enter

what appeared to be a nondescript building. It turned out that they
had my passport, but, when I took a look at it, I saw that it would be
of use only in a government archive. The name on the passport was
mine but the photo was of another gent, far less handsome than yours
truly. The darned thing had been all over the world including, and
one can only imagine the nature of such visits, a whole host of Arab
countries.

I explained my conundrum to a friend of mine who was well
placed in the government and he proposed a solution. He told me to
go to the police chief in Rosh Pina and explain that my home on the
kibbutz suffered a fire and my passport along with all of my personal
papers went up in smoke. When I arrived in Rosh Pina, the police
chief had already been apprised of the situation and had the letter
waiting for me. I was instructed to take the letter to the British consul-
ate in Tel Aviv and ask for a new passport. After doing just that, I was
told to come back in several weeks to pick up my new passport. When
I returned, I was instructed to wait outside the office of the Consul
General. Apparently he wanted to have a few words with me. Finally,
a secretary motioned me in. I noticed that I had entered through the
rear door and that the front door to the office remained firmly closed.
Was this an interrogation of sorts? Well, he handed me the passport
and shook my hand with a firm and unyielding grip. If my palms were
sweaty, he certainly would have noticed. He finally released my hand
and handed me the passport. "Here is your passport, Mr. Nathan. Let
me give you some friendly advice courtesy of Her Majesty's government. Don't ever pull this sort of thing again."

I don't know to this day if the Consul General was aware of my
background and some of my past associations. Something needs to be
said about what may seem to be crafty and even deceitful behavior on
behalf of Israel. The Mossad to this day is forced to do these things
not because it wants to but because it has to. Millions of innocent Jewish lives depend on having the nerve to execute missions that require
one to be less than completely truthful with immigration officials of

I communicated with family back home by writing. I tried to regularly write postcards to the siblings. This one was written sometime before my brother Barry came to Israel in the early 1950s.
(Photo courtesy of Barry Nathan)

various governments. Having access to a variety of passports was and remains vital to secure the survival of Israel. I remember once sitting in the dining room at Kfar Hannasi, sitting with Bobby Rodney. Rodney had come over on Kindertransport and while we were chit chatting over breakfast, the radio was playing in the background. All of a sudden, the news reported that an Israeli spy named Bob Rodney had been executed in Syria. It came as quite a surprise as Bob looked pretty good for a man who had just been killed. Of course, the man who was really executed was the agent who was carrying Bob's passport.

CHAPTER NINE

The Kibbutz Matures

The primary activity of the kibbutzim was agriculture. Two of our biggest problems were the amount and the quality of the land on which we started. You may remember the story of the backbreaking work that it took to clear Mansura al Chait of all of the large rocks. Though we moved the kibbutz to higher ground for security reasons, we continued to work the fields below. Of course, no farmer in his right mind would have done all of that work. It never would have paid. As you have probably figured out, though, our primary motivation in working the land was not to reap financial rewards.

In the 1950s with the draining of the Hula Valley, new farmland became available in what formerly had been a swamp. All of the local kibbutzim received new plots of land and we had to travel some distance to work them. Fortunately, the quality of the land was excellent. It was very fertile and the 250 or so acres that we received were a great asset to us. We were not the only ones who recognized the quality of the land. Some Arabs began to cross over from the Syrian border to avail themselves of this new opportunity. They knew that they weren't supposed to be there and we were able to convince them to return home. The question that remained was what to grow. One of the crops that we introduced was cotton, which became popular not only in the Hula Valley, but throughout Israel. Much of it was exported, but there was a serious problem. Growing cotton requires a huge amount of water, much of it generated through irrigation. It became apparent that the vast majority of our water was going to cotton rather than our other crops, so we had to rethink that decision.

I had a first-hand knowledge of the water situation, since I was responsible for installing the irrigation equipment that we used. I had gotten the plans from the engineers and set up what you would call a pumping station. Israel had become famous for its irrigation technology and several of the kibbutzim took a lead role in its development. One company, Netafim, jointly owned by three kibbutzim, would become a worldwide leader in the field. We employed overhead irrigation, and, as with the fish ponds you are about to hear about, we did all the work at night. We were fighting the power of the sun's rays. We didn't want precious water to evaporate with the heat of the day. We raced to get the water into the ground before the morning sun kicked in.

In addition to our crops, we had livestock and fish ponds. The fish ponds were common among kibbutzim in the north because of the fresh water that flows from the Jordan River. As I am writing this book, there is a big debate going on here in Chicago about how to deal with the Asian carp, a species of fish that is a big problem in Lake Michigan and has a propensity to do what fish are wont to do—eat their fellow fish. We used to stock carp in our fish pond, buying them when they were small and fattening them up. Feeding them entailed rowing out to the middle of the pond and shoveling in large amounts of food. They loved corn. Harvesting them was quite a task. We would then go out at 1:00 in the morning and put them into oxygenated tanks. We then delivered them to the fishmongers in Tel Aviv and Haifa. It was critical that the carp remained alive throughout the journey because that was how the fishmongers sold them to their customers, many of whom were old-fashioned European ladies. I do not know if the carp was then put into the customer's bathtub to swim around in until judgment day, but I do know that they would eventually become gefilte fish. Raising carp was very Jewish work. We harvested twice a year, right before Rosh Hashanah and Pesach. Prices were the highest then for obvious reasons.

The dream of self-sustaining agriculture on kibbutzim never quite worked as envisioned by the Zionist pioneers. The importance of working the land had been drilled into all of us since Habonim. Not being able to work the land for so many years had pushed Jews into unhealthy professions like money-lending. The key to healthy and productive living was getting back to the land. Despite the power of the ideology, however, there were realities to be faced.

It quickly became clear that it was necessary for us to expand beyond farming. As I am fond of pointing out, the kibbutzim were settled based on national goals rather than economic or agricultural ones. Agriculture is always a difficult game. There are so many variables that affect crop production, such as weather and disease. Every farmer in the world has to deal with these things, and what makes it so tough is that you are dealing with nature, which is largely beyond human control. Though Israel became known for its wonderful crops, like the before-mentioned Jaffa oranges, we had plenty of foreign competition. We also had a relatively small amount of land with which to work, and despite all of the success we had enjoyed with irrigation, water and the conflicts with our Arab neighbors surrounding its use remained a problem.

Many of the kibbutzim were to move beyond agriculture into some kind of industrial endeavor. We decided not long after the kibbutz was founded that one of the keys to our long-term economic survival would be to maintain permanent industrial labor on the kibbutz. We looked at different options. One of our members, Yitzchak Minkoff, known to everyone as Minki, had a university degree in metallurgy. He would later leave the kibbutz for a professorship at the Technion to teach that very subject. Another member, Joe Cina, had exposure, through the family business back in England, to metal fabrication.

Speaking to a delegation from Ghana. They were interested in building a foundry. This tour was part of a general Israeli policy of helping newly independent African countries develop economically.

So, in light of these two factors, it was decided that we should build a foundry.

Joe and Minki traveled around the country visiting different foundries. We built ours at the beginning of 1949 in Mansura al Chait and it was a pretty simple facility, using material from Nissan huts and some wood. The whole operation was powered by a 25-horsepower generator. After digging holes in the ground we built a small melting furnace, a kiln, a lathe, with a drill and some tables. What did we cast? At first it was brass joints for sinks and pipes used in homes. How did we get the brass? It was collected from scrap, which included bullet casings, old coins, and other assorted items. After a while, brass soon became very competitive as several other kibbutzim had moved into it. It was decided that we should get into producing aluminum for irrigation pipe fittings.

The Kibbutz Matures

How did we acquire the aluminum? The government had no money to purchase it, so what could we do? We had creative ways of getting what we needed. In a field outside of Sarafand, outside of Tel Aviv, previously the site of a large British army base, there were a lot of old warplanes. Of British, French, and German vintage, they had been brought down during the Second World War and were just sitting there. No one had taken them to the scrap yard so we decided to be the scrap yard. We had to arrange for all of these planes to be brought up to the kibbutz. There we built a furnace out of brick and made a hole about 24 inches wide. We would put the fuselages and engine blocks in, and, due to the extreme heat, the aluminum would simply drop to the bottom. We could not attest to the exact chemical property of the aluminum as we did not have the proper testing equipment. There was plenty of aluminum, at least for a time. Soon enough we would move into stainless steel.

Being creative in scrounging around was not only what we did in the kibbutz but what was done all over Israel. There were limited resources, little money, and few friends around the world to help us. What was junk to others was precious to us. An Israeli businessman found out that there were old International Harvester tractors just sitting and rusting on some Pacific Islands. They had been left there by the American army after it had liberated those islands. It did not pay for the Americans to bring much of their heavy equipment back across the Pacific, so it just sat there until this businessman purchased a bunch of it for $10 a ton and loaded them on a ship bound for Israel. We went to see what he had and bought three of his International Harvester tractors, costing us $1,500. These were three of the best tractors that he had, though they had been rusted and cracked from being exposed to the sea. From the three, I extracted all of the best parts and put together one good tractor. It lasted us a good while.

We moved the original foundry to the current kibbutz site once we received electricity on the kibbutz, sometime around 1952. We started out running on kerosene and then switched to a Buda generator and

Here I am riding the International Harvester Tractor.
This tractor was truly international.

eventually an International Harvester generator before getting hooked up to the to the local power utility. We built a huge furnace, and, by the late 50s, had made contact with a British company named APV which was known to have great expertise with steel casting.

There was a potential impediment to our working with APV. An Arab boycott was in effect, with Israel as the sole focal point. Some companies cooperated with it out of fear of losing their business in the Arab world. Some big American companies, such as Pepsi and McDonald's, would not come to Israel until the 1980s. The idea of a boycott goes back to Mandate Palestine when Arabs leaders tried to prevent their people from buying Jewish goods or patronizing Jewish stores. The boycott intensified after 1948, with most Arab and many Muslim states cooperating with it. A secondary boycott prohibited Arab countries from doing business with foreign companies that had a relationship with Israel. The boycott remains even today though many have opted out. It is a crime in America for a company to cooperate with it. The boycott made it difficult but not impossible for us to reach agreements with foreign companies, but, eventually, we prevailed. Business, after all, is business.

APV agreed to train our workers and several of our guys traveled to England to learn the operation. Joe Cina, Mick Elman, and several others went. We decided to incorporate (so I guess we were capitalists after all) and called our enterprise Habonim Casting Products Ltd. I can't remember if we ever thought of using another name but this one seemed natural enough given our roots. We did fairly well because we were producing a variety of different parts for valves and pumps. As Shmuel Hatzor recently reminded me, we even got an order from the Israeli government for parts that were used in the building of the nuclear reactor in Dimona.

We made the decision that our focus should be on producing ball valves. There are people who are reading this and they are wondering, what in the devil is a ball valve? Well, rather than putting it clumsily into words that may put the reader to sleep, I thought that I would impress my grandchildren and look up the definition of a ball valve on the Internet:

"A ball valve is a valve with a spherical ball, the part of the valve which controls the flow through it. The spherical ball has a hole or port through the middle so that when the port is in line with both ends of the valve, flow will occur. When the valve is closed, the hole is per-pendicular to the ends of the valve, and the flow is

A ball valve

Sthidraulica, Archivo fotográfico
Standard Hidráulica

blocked. The handle or lever will be in line with the port position letting you 'see' the valve's position."

Of course, we had no knowledge of how to produce ball valves. We went to a company in England called Worcester Controls and we wanted to make a know-how agreement with them for us to learn the process. They came back to us and proposed a partnership. We created a company called Worcester Controls Israel, jointly owned. Our foundry would supply all of the machine parts to Worcester Controls Israel which would simply put them together and assemble them. Since our costs were actually quite low, we started exporting the valves back to England.

I realize that I have left out the important details of how I got involved in all of this. The last thing the reader probably remembers regarding my work history was that I was toiling away at the garage at Kfar Giladi and Sonny Weintraub was running for his life. Quite a bit transpired in between that experience and the ball valves. After returning from Kfar Giladi, I was in charge of maintaining all of the equipment on the kibbutz. This I did for several years and I became involved in the factory machinery and eventually worked there full-time. After learning all of the jobs that were performed on the factory floor, I became the production manager.

We were growing sufficiently that we built a new factory and it was time to move our equipment to the new location. I spoke to Frank Waterman, a kibbutz member and the fellow in charge of the physical facility and asked him how long he thought it would take to transfer all of this heavy equipment. Given his limited resources, he told me that it would take him a full week to get the job done. I told him that we could not afford to lose one week's worth of production since we had orders that needed to be filled that week. He told me he was open to any alternatives. I had to figure out a way to get this done quickly, so I donned my thinking cap.

I swiftly concluded that I needed to bring in an outside group of professionals to do the job. Where could I find such men on short notice? I decided not to try the usual commercial movers that could be found in Tel Aviv or Haifa; no time for that. I then remembered that on my many trips to the Haifa port, the stevedores were all Sephardic Jews from the Greek city of Salonika. Some had come to Haifa in the early 1930s and had helped establish Haifa as a Jewish port. Many had been dockworkers for generations and were extremely strong. I approached one of the blokes who looked like he was in charge and explained my predicament. How long would it take his men to move the equipment? He told me that they could do it in a day. So we brought his crew in and you should have seen these guys work. Even Frank Waterman could not believe it. They worked around the clock and the operation did not miss a beat. Thanks to our stevedores from Salonika, we were back in business and filling orders within a day.

As production manager, I learned every aspect of the operation and acquired a level of expertise in the technical aspects of the business. Though I had no formal education, I felt that I could speak the language of metallurgy with anyone in the field. Years later, when I moved to America, I got into a big discussion on a subject in metallurgy with members of the staff at the famed Fermi Labs in Batavia, Illinois. A friendly argument ensued about a technical point. Fermi employs some of the best physicists, engineers, and metallurgists in the country and they were sufficiently impressed by my practical knowledge to ask me to serve on the corrosion committee there, which I did for several years.

From production, I moved into sales. Though I had never thought of myself as a salesman and had not sold anything since the days of helping in my father's clothing store, I did quite well. Perhaps hawking stockings to housewives in Stratford is a bit different than selling ball valves, but many of the principles are the same. I worked hard to learn as much as I could about our customers and established strong relationships with them. In looking at the shelves of our distributors, I could tell them what products they needed to stock. Eventually, they developed great confidence in me.

The original foundry began by employing four kibbutz members, but as we expanded the operation, we realized that the dream of building an industrial base strictly to employ kibbutz members was not working. What was the problem? Not everyone on the kibbutz was suited to or wanted to work in the factory. Perhaps because of the cultural background of our members, they viewed some of the jobs as being hot and dirty. If you have ever been to a foundry, you would certainly agree with that.

I should add that this was and is a problem not just in the kibbutzim but continues to be a serious shortcoming in the state of Israel itself. Much labor, including many construction and service sector jobs, goes to Arabs or foreign workers because Israelis refuse to do them. This is similar to what you see in America today where native-born Americans are not interested in certain kinds of jobs. Most of the construction work in Chicago is done by Mexicans and Eastern European immigrants, so Israel's problems are not unique. The toughest job in the foundry was working the furnace. It was extremely hot. Some of the work, like operating a lathe, was highly repetitive and not considered desirable. Many members wanted to work in the office. Most of the jobs that we needed to fill were not very cushy, so, to avail ourselves of a larger pool of workers, we decided to look outside the kibbutz.

There were members who were dead set against hiring and paying outside workers. To them it smacked of a system that we had to come to Israel to escape. That system was capitalism. Employing outside labor was considered to be exploitative. We would now be bosses. I was one of those who strongly favored hiring outside workers. Why? It was not just a matter of need. The people who constituted our labor pool were predominately immigrants from North Africa and the Middle East. I felt we were helping these people by providing them with good, steady employment. The state had brought these people over and had made certain assurances to encourage immigration. They were promised decent housing and gainful employment. I saw our hiring them as helping to fulfill those promises. More importantly, I saw this as a mitzvah that we needed to perform.

I am pleased to say that, unlike the swimming pool debate, my side won out. It had to win out if the factory was going to operate efficiently. So we began hiring outside workers. While they were originally supposed to supplement the members who were working in the factory, the outside people would eventually become the majority. During the heyday of the operation, we used to bus people in from the town of Hatzor. If you go to the factory today—and the kibbutz has since sold its operation to an outside businessman,—you would be lucky to find a single kibbutz member working in a non-management or office capacity.

I got to know many of these people from Hatzor. Many became my friends. They were very warm folks and very family oriented. Many were quite observant religiously, and even the ones who weren't had great respect for their heritage. They were very different from Ashkenazim. They would invite me to family celebrations. These were wonderful events of a different style than anything I had ever seen before. I was exposed to new traditions, and, of course, new cuisine.

These North African Jews and many others from non-European countries who immigrated to Israel were not always treated well. Their culture was different from ours, and though they would grow to half of the Jewish population in Israel, they were often overlooked. The military and governing elite we spoke about were all either Sabras or had come over as youngsters from Europe. To a person, they were all Ashkenazim. Some looked down on the Sephardic and Oriental Jews. There was considerable prejudice in the air.

I remember the time when my brother-in-law, George Neumark, Mimi's husband, was visiting from Chicago. George was very successful in the diamond business. He was staying at the Tel Aviv Hilton and I went to visit him there. We met in the lobby, and, after speaking for some time, one of his associates came down. After speaking with the gent for a while, it was apparent that something was troubling him. What was it? He told me that his daughter was going to marry a Yemenite man. I thought that was fantastic and figured that as an American he was probably unaware of all of the wonderful traditions for which their culture is known. I told him a little bit about it: the great food, traditional dancing, the magnificent clothing and ornate jewelry, the latter point meant to appeal to his professional sensibilities. I told him a little of their religious and scholarly traditions, traditions that went back over 2,000 years. After I finished my long list of plusses, I noticed he was little impressed. He finally got to his real objection when he told me, "But Alfy, they are colored." I was reminded of the black soldiers whom I had met during the war by the way he said "colored." It was painful to hear someone talk that way about his fellow Jews.

My first experience with Yemenites was most interesting. When we first arrived in Hadera, there was a group of Yemenites who had been living there for some time until more permanent housing was ready for them. We were all living in tents at the time. There was a good deal of tension between our two groups. They had come with their dogs, goats, and sheep and the assorted hoopla made some of our people a bit on edge. Housing was being built for them just outside of Hadera, and, though they were finally ready to move, the Yemenites were hesitant to leave their tents. No doubt they were afraid and who could blame them? Remember, we had spent several years on the Farm to acclimate ourselves to the life that we would be facing. Theirs had been a sudden departure and the journey must have been a harrowing one. While my family had been living in England for around 50 years before I left for Israel, they had been living in Yemen for a few thousand years, often in remote areas. If we thought they dressed, ate, and spoke strangely, can you imagine what they must have made of us?

The housing was finished but the Yemenites were not going anywhere. Finally it was decided that we would have to place them forcibly onto trucks. We hoped that once they saw how nice their new quarters were, they would gladly move in. Well, not quite. I remember the look on their faces. They had never seen indoor plumbing or doors before. The goats took to the indoor plumbing right away, quenching their thirst in the strange looking liquid trough. And the doors? They took them right off the hinges and used them as a roof for their goats. There were many such stories but it all illustrates just how mighty the challenge was in those years. People came from not only Yemen and North Africa but from Turkey, Greece, Iran, Iraq, Bukharia, Russia, Poland, Hungary, and many other places. Some had been to universities and some had never seen a classroom. Some were Chasidic Jews from Transylvania and some were atheists from Budapest. If the kibbutz was a unique social experiment, how much more so was the amalgam that constituted Israeli society in those years?

Part of the reason that the kibbutz was able to stay afloat was due to all the help that the government was providing us with. The Labor Party was in power for the first thirty years of Israel's existence and we were all members or at least were supposed to be loyal party members. We received cheap loans from Bank Hapoalim (the Workers' Bank) whenever we needed capital for housing or other improvement or infrastructure projects. When we needed money to buy livestock or to improve the factory, we could rely on the low interest loans that no private business could get, at least not on the terms that we received.

Although I thought highly of some individual Labor Party leaders, I was not a particularly strong party member. I did not care for the politics of it all. I thought it was largely a waste of time. Nor was I crazy about the Histadrut, the national labor union. They owned many companies like Bank Hapoalim and the game was stacked in our favor. Though I was a member, I did not go along with their agenda. They wanted you to work in the local towns, drumming up support for labor. They wanted you to take an active part in the youth movement, run for political office and the like. It was just not my bag. The kibbutz was often at loggerheads with the local towns, which felt that they were bypassed in favor of the kibbutzim. We got the low interest loans and other perks. We were tied to the elite of the government, the military and the universities. The towns were primarily populated by immigrants, often poor and uneducated. Their interests, unlike ours, were vastly underrepresented in the government.

The whole notion of kibbutz was to be self-sustaining, growing our own food, and providing our own jobs without outside help. It never quite worked that way. We would sell our eggs and then buy eggs for a cheaper price at the market. The same was true of milk. The cows were milked three times a day. It was tough work. Again, we did not drink our own milk. We would sell the milk and buy it back at a cheaper price. The government subsidized bread, milk, and eggs. One does not have to be a Nobel Prize-winning economist to surmise that there was something deeply flawed with the notion that you could buy your own milk and eggs for a cheaper price than you had sold it, but that was how things were done in those days.

These dynamics would all change right after I left Israel when much to everyone's surprise, the opposition took power. Menachem Begin, the man whose face once graced British posters with a byline "Wanted: Dead or Alive," became prime minister after many years of leading that opposition. He did not owe the kibbutzim anything. He owed his election much more to the poorer Oriental and Sephardic Jews who populated the towns. They had supported him and he inaugurated Project Renewal, which sought to improve conditions and create economic opportunities in blighted cities and immigrant towns. Begin was also something of a capitalist though it would take quite an effort to cut into much of the entrenched socialism. The subsidies to the kibbutzim were decreased and eventually eliminated. The banks began lending money like banks do in most countries, with the interest rate in proportion to the credit worthiness of the borrower. The relationship of the town to the kibbutz changed. Eventually, the kibbutz would turn to the town to help provide jobs for its members.

I would travel all over the country selling, but I did much of my business in Tel Aviv. I was frequently away for a good portion of the

At a trade show in Tel Aviv speaking with Pinchas Sapir,
who served terms as both Minister of Finance and Minister of
Trade and Industry. L to r, Pinchas Sapir (with glasses), me,
Michael Cohen, Henry Ben Yehuda. (Courtesy of Sheila Ben Yehuda)

week. Of course, the travel schedule was not beneficial to family life. I was coming back with orders, however, and felt I was doing much to benefit the kibbutz. One day, I was sitting around having dinner with several other people, and the conversation as usual turned to the various daily problems we were experiencing on the kibbutz. One of my friends turned to me and said, "It is all right for you. What do you have to worry about it? You are away all week enjoying yourself."

I was a bit surprised by the comment and the obvious sentiment behind it. I thought there would be appreciation for what I was doing, but a level of jealousy had crept in, at least among some. Of course, I was not benefiting materially from my efforts so you would have

Toasting to our success at a restaurant in the Yemenite quarter of Tel Aviv. L to r, me, Betty Doary, Osssy Edelstein, Rueven Gutta, Michael Doary, Henry Ben Yehuda. (Courtesy of Sheila Ben Yehuda)

thought there would be little to be jealous about. Despite our lofty goals, it appeared that jealousy was tough to root out among humans, having been around since Cain and Abel. One area of friction revolved around the car, in this case, the one that belonged to the factory. People would sign it out. I needed the car to be well maintained and clean. How could I tell a customer that the seat was sticky because Chaim or Shlomo had spilled a Coke and neglected to clean it up?

When I was going to Eilat or Tel Aviv, there were always people who wanted a ride. Sometimes the person was going on vacation. Usually members received two weeks of vacation, and vacations on the kibbutz were a little bit different than what they would be outside of it. The kibbutz would have an arrangement with a particular hotel and would have a room rented for the use of the kibbutz. A new person would arrive every week or so and take his vacation there. Where would he eat? There would be a similar arrangement with a restaurant so the person would eat there. Eventually, people became dissatisfied with this system. They grew tired of returning to the same place, of eating in the same restaurant. Sometimes they wanted to go visit their relatives. They preferred cash to coupons. They wanted to take their vacation when and where they saw fit. Relatives of kibbutz members would come to visit Israel, sometimes staying at fine hotels. They would want their children and grandchildren to stay with them there. One acquired a taste of what it is like to stay at a Sheraton or a Hilton.

People received a stipend with which to buy clothes. Again, the idea was to lessen inequality by having everyone basically wearing the same type of clothes. In the early days, that was fine. Everyone was too consumed by the challenges of basic survival to think too much about these matters. When things improved, however, it became clear that some people were more interested in their wardrobe than others. I was never much interested in clothes. I still own some shoes from my kibbutz days. They are considerably older than many people I know. I have been teased over the years for some of my apparel choices, like my infamous orange shirt. Eventually, people demanded the cash to spend as they pleased. The whole premise of a kibbutz society is the ability to surrender individual desires for the greater good of the collective, but individuality and individual desires run strong in some folks.

I was most anxious to make the Habonim Company as profitable as possible. I felt that one of the limitations that we faced was in having to sell through our distribution network. It seemed to me that we could do better by selling directly to the buyer and I proposed cutting out the middle man. I had a whole plan set up, had warehouse space picked out in Tel Aviv, and introduced the ideas to some of the decision makers of the kibbutz. I thought that people would see the light, would realize that it was the way to go. I was confident we could pull it off. Instead, people were upset with me. One of my friends said to me, "We came here to build up the country, not to be Sochrim (business people)." I suppose this is what really bothered them. By selling the product directly, we were inching ever slowly to capitalism. We were selling out our ideals. Ironically, the kibbutz would eventually take my suggestion many years later but it was not ready to accept the reality that its members were at least de facto capitalists. For me, this should have been the moment that I realized that my days on the kibbutz were numbered, but, frankly, I didn't. I still loved many aspects of the kibbutz.

It is quite possible that there were other people who started to sense some of my reservations. One of my pet peeves were the endless meetings. The main structure upon which decisions are made on the kibbutz is the General Assembly, which would meet every Saturday night. As I had mentioned earlier, it was probably closest to the town meeting format that has become popular in recent years here in America. The difference was that there was real power in the General Assembly. That is not to say that there was no formal leadership on the kibbutz. A secretary was elected and he would essentially direct the meeting. Every aspect of kibbutz life could not be covered in these meetings, however long they lasted. That was where the committees came into play. There were the Economics Committee, the Works Committee, the Agricultural Committee, and the Education Committee. There were even the Social Committee and the Vacation Committee.

These committees would meet and present issues to be voted on during the General Assembly. Everyone has an equal vote, and, to my way of thinking, that was part of the problem. When I was working in the garage, we needed a new combine. Yet the purchasing decision was made by individuals who barely knew what a combine was. I understood the ideological basis for every member having a vote, but I felt that individuals who had responsibilities for different functions on the kibbutz should be entrusted with greater autonomy. While it was never easy, direct democracy through the General Assembly was manageable when the kibbutz was relatively small. Once membership ballooned into the hundreds, it became far more difficult.

The Kibbutz Matures

Many of the meetings would drag on. To me, they became a waste of time. I felt that many people talked for the purpose of airing a grievance that was important to that individual, but did not require the participation of the entire kibbutz. There were other aspects of the General Assemblies that bothered me. There were a few folks who were blessed with the gift of gab. If they were good talkers and were persistent, they could force others to vote for what they wanted by pushing their agenda. People just tired of resisting whatever it was they were advocating. Eventually, I grew frustrated enough by the meetings that I started attending less and less often. I am sure that there were people who did not appreciate my absence.

Despite my frustration, or perhaps because of it, I was given an exciting assignment. In 1965, I was given an opportunity by the central kibbutz organization to which Kfar Hanassi belonged. I was to go to England to run an office that was in charge of marketing the products for all of the kibbutzim that were members of the federation. We spent two years in London, living first in an apartment over a beauty salon that was owned by my sister, Kit, and her husband. We then moved into a beautiful home in the neighborhood of Eltham.

Part of the reason I was sent to England was that exporting was not working well financially for the kibbutzim. The agents and distributors had taken so much money out of the deal that there was precious little left for the kibbutzim. I was going to cut out the middle man by setting up contact between the kibbutzim and the end user of the product. It ended up quite well as I was able to create agreements with British customers. Some of the products I was promoting, like the irrigation equipment, were cutting edge. There was a kibbutz in Israel that manufactured a plastic chicken crate. It was cast with a huge die, the biggest one ever made for plastics, and there came a time when they were exporting them in the hundreds. These crates were very good for sterilization, a great improvement over the wooden chicken crates. With those wooden crates, there was always a great danger of bacteria, something the plastic chicken crates largely eliminated.

The plastic chicken crates were made by kibbutz Maagen Michael. This kibbutz is located to the south of Haifa, and is the largest and one of the most successful in Israel. Though the kibbutz was founded in its current location in 1949, it had set up shop in Rehovot several years before that. Though it was operating a laundry which pressed the uniforms of British soldiers, "Kibbutz Hill" as it was called, was up to something besides steam cleaning. It had a secret Haganah munitions factory on premises, manufacturing ammunition for Sten machine guns. It was all top secret; the workers were not allowed to reveal a thing. The British never discovered the secret entrance to the factory. Louie and Sheila Ben Yehuda worked there, producing ammo. Today, a museum operates where the ammo was once produced, to educate people about its history.

The most difficult aspect of any move is uprooting children from school and friends. In this case, it was made even more severe by the fact that the girls were leaving their country and the kibbutz. The girls managed to adjust to their new circumstances quite well. Due to the school that she was attending in England, Rena found her calling in art. She went to an art school in London and even stayed on in England after we had returned to Israel.

I was in England during the Six Day War, and though I tried to return, it was not possible. When I finally returned to Israel, the map had changed. With our great victory, we now controlled all of Jerusalem, the Sinai desert, the Gaza Strip, the West Bank, and, of course, the Golan Heights. We were no longer on the border. There was a significant buffer between us and Syria. I had completed my reserve army duties before I had left for England. The Israeli armed forces had performed spectacularly well during the war. It was considered one of the greatest victories in the annals of modern warfare. Despite this, the IDF is not known for handing out a lot of combat ribbons and medals the way most Western militaries do. As a citizen army, everyone is expected to do their part. Only in cases of exceptional valor are decorations awarded.

Our house in Eltham, in the London borough of Greenwich.
A HIllman Minx motor car is in the driveway.

I have combat ribbons from the British army but the only award which I hold dear was awarded to me in 1968 as part of a twenty-year celebration of the State. Those who had participated in illegal immigration were invited to Haifa Port, which had been closed off for the occasion. The event was sponsored by the Port and the Zim Shipping Company. Those of us in attendance were treated to a reenactment of some episodes from Mossad LeAliyah Bet operations in Italy and France. It was quite a spectacular event and was very moving. As a veteran of the Palyam, I was fortunate, along with many others, to receive a bronze medal in recognition of my service during Aliyah Bet. My daughter,

Rena, was sitting with me as we were watching the reenactment. She had heard stories over the years, but when she saw some of the events that I had spoken about with her own eyes, it became very real.

Eventually I moved into international sales for Habonim. It was a natural outgrowth of my success in London and I began to travel throughout the world. Sometimes I participated in an Israeli industrial exhibition. I traveled to Iran on such a venture. In today's climate, we think of Iran together with Holocaust denial, show trials of Jews, and worries about Iran's nuclear capabilities. It is very interested in wiping out Israel. Those who are young may not remember that at one time the two countries enjoyed excellent relations. The Shah treated the large Persian Jewish community well and they were very fond of him. As Israelis, we were well received in Iran, but the government had asked us not to fly the Israeli flag at our booth. Despite their strong relationship with us, they were worried about criticism among their neighbors. I remember being greatly impressed with the country, its beautiful buildings, museums, and cafes. We were doing a lot of work there, but I did not come back with any orders.

A number of years later, I was asked to be part of an Israeli delegation that was putting on a show of Israeli products in Bucharest, Romania. We were trying to get our products into Eastern Europe, and, though our relations were very bad with the Soviet Union at the time, that was not the case throughout the Eastern Bloc. I remember that part of the trade fair centered on the books that we were exhibiting. We were told not to show anything dealing with the Israeli-Arab conflict, only Jewish books. I still remember the faces of the many Jews of Bucharest who had come to our booth. Many had survived the war and were most anxious to visit us. By the end of the exhibition, the pages of the books were discolored from people leafing through them.

It was quite an education being in Bucharest. You saw up close how an oppressive communist regime operated. We had smuggled in past Romanian customs officials single recordings of the famous song, "Jerusalem of Gold." We hoped that they would find their way into

Jewish hands and not into the possession of the Romanian secret police. I doubt they would have enjoyed it very much or appreciated the sentiments behind this marvelous song. We met Jews in Bucharest, but were instructed by our own people to meet them in public places, such as hotel lobbies, so that they would suffer no recriminations from the authorities. The idea was not to go to their homes. Of course, you knew you were being followed. We did not use the phones in the hotel, only public telephones. We were also instructed that if we became ill that we should leave the country, not go to the hospitals. They were all run by the government and the secret police could come in and drug you. Just as in my days in France during illegal immigration, there was a little danger.

I was already divorced by now. Those of us who were single used to take some of the lovely local girls around the shows. We took turns and I gave a nice tour of our different exhibits to this charming blonde woman. In making conversation, I was invited to dinner. She picked me up at the hotel in a black car. In those days, only the government and army people drove black sedans. Although the evening was pleasant enough, I thought something was up and got in touch with our embassy people. They informed me that she was the daughter of a prominent general who had apparently fallen out of favor with the regime. I made sure to stay away. I had already had my fill of international intrigue.

Though I had gotten orders from countries all over the world, I couldn't seem to break through in Bucharest. We were not selling to industrial companies, but, rather, all of the buying was handled through central purchasing offices. I thought I had good products, but came back empty handed. Finally, I was on a plane coming back from another unsuccessful trip and ran into a fellow Brit who was doing a robust trade with Bucharest. I explained my predicament.. "How did you do it?" I asked him. He told me, "Alfy, when you go there, take a brown envelope with some jewelry or perfume and place it in on the desk of the secretary. Tell her who you are interested in seeing. It

Shaking hands with President Katzir after receiving award on behalf of Habomin. It reads, *Outstanding Exporter, Metals Division.*

should get you an order." I was a little bit shocked. Of course, this was just how business was done in Eastern Europe at the time.

I was now an international traveler. In addition to my trips to Western and Eastern Europe, I began to travel the Americas, both North and South. We were doing business all over the world. The crowning moment came when I won the award for the metals division as "Exporter of the Year." This award came from the Ministry of Trade and I was presented it by the President of the State of Israel, in this case, Ephraim Katzir. As export manager, I was very happy, but, Alfy Nathan, the person, was not so happy and would soon export another product from Israel, namely himself.

PART FOUR

A New Adventure

CHAPTER TEN

The Decision to Leave

If each chapter of my life, like each chapter of this book, represents a distinct phase in my life, then making the decision to leave the kibbutz was the most arduous of all. It was an extremely difficult decision to make and I spent hours mulling it over in my head. I thought about it and re-thought about it, but, no matter how many times it percolated in my brain, no matter how many different angles I looked at it, no matter how many times I weighed the pros and the cons, it came up the same each time. The right thing to do, perhaps the *only* thing to do, was to leave.

The reader may be a little confused at this point. He or she may want to put the book down and call me on the phone to ask, "But, Alfy, you put so much of yourself into the kibbutz, your family was there, and besides all of that, you loved the state of Israel, believed deeply in it, and took great pride in its many achievements. How could you just pick up and leave?" It is a good question and is worthy of an explanation.

The genesis of my decision dates back to 1965, when my family and I spent two years on England. For me, it was a very good experience. I felt that I was being successful, accomplishing much for the kibbutz movement as a whole. I say the kibbutz movement because I am referring to individual kibbutzim whose products I was promoting. These kibbutzim were marketing everything from toilets to plastic chicken crates.

It was an ideal assignment for me and I have always had a suspicion that perhaps I was sent to England because there were those who felt that I was already becoming disenchanted with kibbutz life and this was the best way to keep me interested. They were not wrong. Of course, I thought it a bit ridiculous that I was posted there for only two years. It took two years just to gain the trust and confidence of my British clients. There was probably something else at work here. Perhaps hindsight is indeed 20/20, but, in looking back on it all, I think once I got a bit of a taste for capitalism, I wanted more. My entrepreneurial fire may have gotten a bit stoked in those days because I thought about staying in England past my two-year term and starting my own business. For some reason, I felt that a dump truck business suited me. If you remember, I had been driving a truck since the war and felt I could do well in this business. My brother, Sid, after discussing it with me, talked me out of it. He felt it was just too big of a risk. Perhaps it was not the right time for me and I heeded his advice.

The person who was most against staying in England, even if it was not going to be a permanent move, was Louie. A chasm was growing ever wider between the two of us. It revolved around the way we felt about the kibbutz. Louie was, as they say, a "true believer." When I started voicing my concerns to her about certain aspects of kibbutz life or its administration, she invariably sided with the kibbutz. More than anything, she deeply loved the kibbutz. She would work in the kitchen, cooking for hundreds of people. She would sing in the choir and her beautiful paintings proudly adorned the walls of the children's home. She was selfless in all she did on behalf of the kibbutz. It gave her enormous satisfaction.

Although I headed back to Israel, and while I had some very successful years working for Habonim, my disenchantment only grew stronger. While I was still a member of the kibbutz, I always felt it was very important not to be negative in any way. You had to give it your all. If you could not do that, then you should leave. I was finding it ever more difficult to follow my own advice.

My marriage to Louie would end in divorce. Like every divorce, there are two sides to the story, but the bottom line was it failed. I accept responsibility for that failure. Louie has since passed away and the last thing I would want to do would be to tarnish her memory. She was a wonderful woman, but our differences proved too significant to sustain the marriage. It was all very unfortunate, and, of course, my greatest concern was how it would affect my two daughters.

Getting a divorce is an awful ordeal to go through at any time and in any place, but, certainly, getting divorced on a kibbutz at that stage of my life only compounded all of the negatives. For the first time in many, many years, I found myself alone. The kibbutz simply was not a good place for that. Trying to restore a social life in early middle age was going to be near impossible there. I was considering leaving. Many of my friends tried to talk me out of it. They took turns working on me, hoping that one of them would eventually get through and I would see the light. I was, after all, doing the unthinkable—walking away. You can't blame them for wanting me to stay. You have to remember that the kibbutz predated the year 1948. It originated as a dream spoken about in Habonim meetings in London and then was forged into a reality on the David Eder Farm. I was considering making a break with that dream—with that ideal.

It is true that there were many things with which I was unhappy. Some dealt with practical issues such as the governance of the kibbutz, to which I have previously alluded. Others were personal. I mentioned that Rena had stayed in England and attended art school there. When she came back to Israel she served in the army and eventually studied at Bezalel Academy of Art and Design, Israel's national art school. One day she was waiting for a bus to take her to school when she met Sefi Rivlin, who was then a young acting student. You never know what can happen when you are waiting for a bus, and, in this case, Rena met the man who would become her husband. Sefi comes from a prominent family, the Rivlins being related to the Vilna Gaon, the 18th century Talmudic luminary and leader of non-Chassidic Jewry. Sefi's ancestor, Binyamin Rivlin, a student of the Gaon's, came to Palestine in the early 19th century and helped build up the Jewish community of Jerusalem.

Sefi and Rena did not have any great desire to live on the kibbutz. Sefi had not grown up on one and his politics were hardly labor zionist. One of his relatives serves the present government as the Minister of Communications and his family includes strong Likud people. This did not make him tremendously popular at Kfar Hanassi, and when Rena decided well before her marriage that she was going to get a place in town, all the kibbutz would provide her with was a mattress. This did not make me terribly happy.

I was somewhat ambivalent when Rena became engaged. After all, Sefi was at the time a struggling actor. He had no money, but, of course, neither did I. Little did I know that he would one day become one of Israel's most beloved actors. To this day, whenever I meet Israelis they all recognize his name; he is a true celebrity.

The wedding date was set but the kibbutz felt that since she had already left the kibbutz, she was effectively on her own. It was not interested in contributing toward the wedding. I was quite angry and went to some of the leaders and told them, "Listen, between Louie and me, the two of us have spent 50 years on this kibbutz and we can't do anything to give our daughter a decent wedding?" I felt that the fact that she was our daughter should have bestowed upon the kibbutz some level of responsibility. The reason we could not afford to make the wedding was because we had joined the kibbutz. We effectively had no private funds of our own. Eventually, the kibbutz decided that it would provide transportation for people on the kibbutz who were coming to the wedding. It also agreed to provide some fresh fruit, but the whole episode upset me a great deal. It pained to me to think that

Rena in her army uniform.

My younger daughter, Yael.

The Decision to Leave

I had no resources of my own to help my two daughters very much. In twenty years, I could picture myself as a pensioner, just barely getting by and growing old most ungracefully. It was not a pretty picture. If I wanted to avoid that fate, I would have to take action and I would have to take it soon.

My younger daughter, Yael, after finishing high school, went into the army. I was very proud when she became an officer. Later, she would go to school and become a nurse. While in the army, she met a young, handsome medic who was serving with an airborne unit. Alex Winkler, like many Jews of his generation, came from a family of Holocaust survivors. His father came from Hungary and endured the horrors of a concentration camp. Like many survivors' families, his wife and children had been killed and he set out to try to begin life anew.

Mr. Winkler had remained in Hungary and started a company that manufactured luggage, but, when the Soviets began to tighten their noose, he left the country and closed up his factory. He simply walked away, padlocking his factory and telling people he was going to Paris for the weekend. With the Soviet oppression, which included mass arrests, persecutions, and executions, he reasoned that he had had enough. I remember he told me when explaining his decision to leave, "I was not going to lose another family," and he stayed in Paris for a year before he made his way to Israel. He started over again, opening a dry cleaning business in Tel Aviv where he spent nearly two decades before coming to Vancouver and starting from scratch one last time.

I was on the road a good deal for Habonim and would come back to my empty bachelor quarters. By 1976, I made the decision to leave the kibbutz. The most logical place to go would be Tel Aviv, a very cosmopolitan city and a major center for business. I had an excellent relationship with our main distributor there, and reasoned that I would have no trouble securing employment with him. I spoke to the head man and he was very excited to bring me on. After all, after so many years of working together, I knew his business almost as well as he did. Then, shortly before I was going to work for him, he told me that he could not hire me. What happened? Someone from the kibbutz had spoken with him and told him that if he hired me, the kibbutz would not do business with him. Why did someone, presumably a friend, do that to me? It was not to hurt me, God forbid. He thought that blocking my move would keep me on the kibbutz. If I had no alternative, he reasoned, I would grit my teeth and make the best of it. He figured wrong.

Given the nature of my business contacts, I reached the conclusion that wherever I went to work in Israel, I would always be looking over my shoulder. Israel is, after all, a very small country in more than just its land mass. I felt that if I could not work in Israel, I could not stay there. I started to explore other options. I had contacts all over the world and some of my customers had hinted in the past that if I were ever interested, they would like to hire me. I received two offers: one from London and one from Antwerp. London seemed to be a natural. I had three siblings there and a good number of friends and business contacts. As you have no doubt gathered from this book, I spoke the language as well. Of course, Antwerp did not sound bad either. It is a beautiful city with a strong Jewish community. Each city had the advantage of being only about 2,000 miles or so from Israel, allowing me to visit regularly.

There was another option to consider. I had been doing a fair amount of business for the kibbutz in the United States. Perhaps it was worth thinking about the New World. My sister, Mimi, had married an American, George Neumark, and was living in Chicago. My father, if you remember from the very beginning of this book, was the oldest in his family and came to London by himself, and, after establishing himself, decided to remain there while his parents and sisters immigrated to New York City. His parents had long since passed away and he had not seen his sisters in fifty years. One of them was born in America and he had never met her. So, in the 1950s, he set out from London on the Queen Mary and journeyed across the ocean. It was quite a scene when he got off the boat in New York. Can you imagine not seeing your sisters for fifty years? It was such an unusual reunion that one of the newspapers in New York had done a human interest story on it complete with a photograph of the happy scene. My father then went to Chicago and spent time with Mimi and George and their family.

I had taken my first trip to America to join Dad on his historic journey. Air travel was different in those days. There were no supersonic jets. I went to Ireland and from there we did not go straight to New York, but, rather, stopped in Newfoundland, the most eastern point of Canada, to refuel before landing in the United States. I had always liked the States and had a customer in Chicago named Bert Warshaw. He was one of those people who had intimated to me that if I ever wanted to leave Israel, I should call him. It was not an ironclad guarantee, but I felt good about it. I contacted Mimi and informed her that I was weighing either Chicago or London. She encouraged me to come and told me that her home was open to me and I was welcome to stay as long as I needed. Though I probably would not have gone had my sister not been living there, I made the decision to come to America largely based on economic criteria. My gut sense was that the economy was simply better there and though the mid-to-late 70s was a tough time in the United States, I felt that its economic future was brighter than Europe's.

Though I had rationalized it all, leaving was still very rough. I was leaving a country that I deeply loved. I was leaving friends and the only life I knew. I remember the tears that I shed during the long flight to America. I mostly thought of my two daughters, how I was going to miss them, not knowing when I would see them again. I decided to go with a one-way ticket. That way, if things got tough as they no doubt would, I would not be able to pack up and head home.

Sometimes when I fly internationally, I am amazed at how much luggage people bring with them. People may be going for a short visit but it looks like they have stuffed everything into their suitcases but the kitchen sink. Apparently they don't want to be caught without their favorite sweater or pair of trousers. I did not bring all that much with me for one very simple reason: I did not own very much. My net worth was zilch and I had few possessions. The kibbutz bought my ticket and gave me a little bit of spending money, but I had little else except the shirt on my back and a few other garments as well. I stopped off in London to visit family and my brother, Sid, lent me 500 pounds sterling. It was a good amount and when I tried to pay him back once I got on my feet, he told me that I should use the money to help another family member, which I did.

I must make a full admission. Though I had carried a briefcase full of francs in Marseilles and closed big business deals for Habonim, I had never before written a check. I was a quick study, though, and in the years that would follow, I would become something of an expert in this area. Though I knew not what the future would bring when I landed in Chicago's mammoth O'Hare International Airport, I knew one thing for sure: it was not likely to be dull.

Mimi and George were glad to see me and their kindness and love really helped sustain me as I got settled. You may remember that George was in the diamond business. He is not a native Chicagoan. He grew up in New York and after a stellar academic record, came to Chicago first for his studies, matriculating at the University of Chicago. He would go on to earn a master's degree there. He became an officer in the United States Army Air Corps, serving in the war and then serving as in the reserves for many years before retiring as a lieutenant colonel in the Air Force. His family, originally from Eastern Europe, had gone into the diamond business while living in Antwerp. His grandfather had come over to America to set up a branch of the business and died while coming back to Europe aboard the Lusitania, forcing George's father to come to America to take over the operation. While in graduate school, George had sold some diamonds, and, enjoying success, decided to open a branch of the family's business in Chicago. George and Mimi had three children and two of them were in high school when I came to town. All three would go on to become prominent professors, a most unusual achievement.

Together with my brother-in-law, George Neumark,
in front of his Skokie home.

My sister Mimi is a most elegant lady, extremely well-mannered and highly cultured. It is hard to believe we were raised in the same family though I am sure she has had an edifying influence on me. When I came to Chicago, I did not own a suit and was not terribly fond of neckties. The High Holidays were not far off and Mimi insisted that I get a decent suit and tie. I remember going down to Irv's Men's Shop, a fantastic menswear store, and picked up both pieces of clothing. I looked a lot less like a kibbutznik once I put that suit on; the necktie completely belied my background.

1976 was the Bicentennial year in America. I arrived in the summer just in time to view the celebration. Though America was celebrating its independence from my country of origin, I did not feel any hostility in the air. If anything, people seemed to welcome immigrants, just as they had been doing since the country's inception. There were so many things that were different. The first thing that hit me was the vastness of the country. I was coming from Israel, which is somewhere around the size of the state of New Jersey, and this was quite a change. The greater Chicago area was enormous, with a population larger than Israel's. The number and variety of people were not the only differences. When I walked into the supermarket, I could not believe the variety of foods that you could buy. There were even so many different brands of butter and margarine. There were times when I would just look around it all, as if in a state of child-like amazement. I remember the first time that I went to one of the big car dealers in the suburbs. I looked out at the behemoth lot. There were cars for as far as the eye could see. It seemed to be as though there were more cars in that one lot than there were in all of Israel. A land of plenty, this United States of America.

The first thing I did after unpacking was to call Bert Warshaw. Bert ran a company called Stainless Piping Materials, and, as the name suggests, he was in the stainless steel piping equipment business. We had done business when I was working at Habonim and he seemed pleasantly surprised by my call. He greeted me warmly and before I could even ask him for a job, he wanted to know when I could start. I told him the very next day. Bert's office and warehouse were in the city, located at 2600 West Lake Street in the Humboldt Park neighborhood on Chicago's West Side. Though Humboldt Park had been named for Alexander Von Humboldt, a Prussian naturalist, it was not exactly a nature preserve. It was more of a jungle. Though first a German neighborhood and then Jewish, the famous Jewish writer Saul Bellow having grown up there, by the time I showed up, it was primarily Puerto Rican. The area had been the scene of riots in the 60s, and by the 70s, there was plenty of gang and drug activity to be found. Parking was always difficult. There were plenty of no-parking zones, and it was rumored that, in true Chicago fashion, certain officials had been paid off to allow us to park there. Even if you found a space, your car was never safe. I remember once getting a call from an irate person in the neighborhood telling me that our company car was in his driveway. I said, "No it can't be." He told me to look out the window and sure enough, he was right. It was our car, or, I should say it was a skeleton of what the car had once been, stripped down, its radio, tires and nearly everything else gone.

There were many times in my life when I had to have my wits about me. In Normandy and Marseilles it was crucial, and certainly in the early years of the kibbutz when our security situation was tenuous, it was critical. Now I needed to have my wits about me while walking around Humboldt Park. There was more to be worried about than just roaming gangs looking to relieve you of your valuables. There were two black Doberman pinscher dogs which guarded our warehouse. Was I glad once they got used to my scent! I was more worried about them than about the Syrian troops from my kibbutz days. Though unarmed, the Dobermans were a lot meaner.

Despite the location, the job went well. I received a number of promotions and soon enough would find myself as vice president of sales. That was not the only part of my life that was going well. I had been divorced now for nearly two years, and, as you can imagine, people had taken to fixing me up. Mimi was very active in B'nai Emunah, a synagogue in Skokie and was friendly with the rebbetzin there, Miriam Stern. Miriam had thought of fixing me up with one of the synagogue members with whom she was very close and whom Mimi knew as well. Miriam wanted to run it by my sister to see what she thought;

Mimi did not hold out much hope. She questioned whether I was good enough for the fine lady in question, but I was given her number anyway and she was expecting a call from me. I had been in the country for only about a month and since things were going well, I was preparing to move out of Mimi's home and into an apartment on Sheridan Road on the north side of the city. It was an area that I considered the best for single people, but after I called the woman whose name I had been given, I knew I would not be unattached indefinitely.

There really is not a lot of mystery here about the woman whom I was about to call since I have been referring to Lil throughout the course of this book. Well, I phoned her up and asked her out on a date. We were having trouble coming up with a mutually convenient time. Lil was a busy lady with a lot of commitments. Like me, she was divorced with daughters; in her case, she had three. To say she was hard working, is to understate the matter. A Brooklyn native, Lil had to come to Chicago with her ex-husband not long after they were married. She had an uncle who had come to Chicago years earlier from New York and established himself as a businessman. Lil's husband had gone to work for her uncle. Lil had been graduated with an education degree from Brooklyn College and had worked as a teacher before starting a family. She had gone back to work when the girls got older and was teaching at a middle school. She also took on a part-time afternoon job as an insurance underwriter with a local firm to help make ends meet. If that was not enough to keep the average person busy, she had started a business as a wedding planner/consultant, too, so she was frequently working nights and weekends.

As her wedding business picked up and became steady, she would eventually quit her other jobs. One of the things that most impressed me about Lil was her initiative. Like me, she had gone through hard times and had suffered through a divorce, but she was not one to complain or feel sorry for herself. That was evident from our first date. Oh, what about that first date? I would like to say that it was an extremely romantic night out on the town, but it was not. I needed to get some furniture for my new place and was going to an estate sale where I was hoping to pick up a few pieces. Lil helped me pick up a nice chair and we still have it in our home. I must mention one other thing about that first date. I did not yet have a nice car so I asked my boss if I could borrow his car for the occasion. He happily obliged but I called Lil before I came over to explain the circumstances. The car was a shiny Cadillac and I felt it would misleading for her to believe that it was mine. I did not want her to think that I was anyone but Alfy, a recent immigrant who was in the process of establishing himself in a new country. Apparently, my disclosure impressed her and it was a major selling point as she agreed to go out a second time. This time I took her out for a decent meal.

Lil was taking a liking to me; of that I was pretty sure. There was more to winning her over, though, since I had to endear myself to the three young ladies whose lovely mother they were naturally expected to protect. Her oldest daughter, Sherry, was married and living in a nearby suburb. Her middle daughter, Robin, was away at university; in her case, quite far away in Moscow—no, not Moscow, Russia, but Moscow, Idaho. Her youngest daughter, Laurie, who would be my toughest sell, was at home finishing high school. Eventually, I was able to win her over although it was not easy. It took time for her to get used to me. That is only natural. It was much easier for the other two. Years later while celebrating an anniversary, Robin had framed for us a letter that she had received from her mother soon after we had begun dating. (Our grandchildren and great-grandchildren may be surprised to learn that once upon a time people actually sat down with pen and paper and wrote letters.) Interspersed with all of the other news at the time, Lil had written these words: "Had another date last night with a guy named Alfy. He is from Israel and used to live on a kibbutz. Found him to be very interesting. I hope to see him again."

See me again she would, and it became very apparent to the two of us that we had a future together. One day I received a call from Ron Kersten, an old contact of mine who was based in Los Angeles. He had planned to set up a new company, and wanted me as a partner. I told him I would have to think it over. It was an exciting opportunity. I liked and trusted Ron. There was just one problem. I needed to move to Los Angeles but would only consider going if Lil would come with me. I discussed it with her over dinner and she told me that she could not make such a move at the time. It would be too disruptive. I appreciated that she was thinking about her children first and called Ron to tell him that for personal reasons, I could not accept his offer. My relationship with Lil was just too important to me.

CHAPTER ELEVEN

Building a Company

In the United States, I learned that there is something called the "American Dream." To many people it means that in America one can reach whatever height one's ambition, talent, and hard work will allow. One is not stuck in a caste or a class as in many societies. It is a free enterprise system or at least has been so until fairly recently. It rewards risk takers: men like Thomas Edison and Bill Gates. Most immigrants don't dream of becoming Bill Gates. They dream that one day they will become their own boss, even if that means they are a boss only over themselves. Well, around the same time that Bill Gates started the company that would one day be Microsoft, I was getting ready to start my own firm, one that would be considerably smaller but no less important to me as Microsoft is to Gates.

Why did I want to start my own company? It is a logical question to ask. Unlike Thomas Edison or Bill Gates, I did not have dreams of a new invention changing the world or revolutionizing the way business is conducted. I simply had tired of making money for other people, of working hard and not receiving what I felt I was due. On the kibbutz, I did not expect to benefit materially from my work. That was part and parcel of what it meant to be a kibbutznik. Even while working for Bert Warshaw, I felt I was still limited in terms of advancement and remuneration despite the fancy title that I had acquired. It is true that I was a vice president of sales, but I was vice president of sales for someone else. Bert had brought his daughter and son-in-law into the business. Guess who was assigned the informal task of training them? You guessed it: Alfy Nathan. If I stayed at Stainless Piping Materials long enough, I would eventually be reporting to both of them. That prospect did not thrill me.

They say timing is everything. Was this the right time to start a business? After all, I had a good job, was doing pretty well, and I was getting ready to marry Lil. I also did not have a lot of money in the bank, nor the traditional means at my disposal of getting start-up money. So how practical was my plan? I felt deep down in my gut that I could pull it off. Now it was time to find out if Lil felt the same way about my prospects. When I apprised her of my intentions, the first thing she wanted to know was if I was crazy. Perhaps I was, because, as she rightly pointed out, men in their mid-50s do not usually go into business for the first time. They are more likely to be winding down a bit, perhaps working on their golf game. I was headed in the other direction. I also knew that most new businesses did not make it to the first year. Bankruptcy did not frighten me. I had been through so much in life that there was very little left to scare me. Perhaps Lil sensed that. She is a very perceptive woman and could see that no matter what the obstacles, I was determined to try my luck, even if it meant going it alone. She not only pledged her support, but would play an integral role in making my fledgling enterprise a success. From the beginning, we saw this as something we were doing together.

There was only one person who needed to be informed of my plans: Bert Warshaw. As I mentioned, I was grateful to Bert but felt that I had paid him back by bringing in a lot of business. Both Lil and I wanted to remain on good terms with Bert so we thought the best thing to do would be to invite him and his family for a nice dinner before breaking the news to him. I was not sure how he was going to take it. I also knew that it was inevitable that some of the business that I had brought to his firm would follow me to my new company. That is the nature of business. We broke the news to Bert over a glass of wine and he wished me well; he even proposed a toast to my success. Not that he did not try to keep me on. He even offered to trade the company car that I was using, which was a less appealing brown station wagon, for a nice Ford Thunderbird as an incentive to stay. I thanked him for hiring me when I first came to America and told him that I had hoped we could remain on good terms and become friendly competitors. Bert agreed, but it did not quite work out that way.

If you have been reading this book from the beginning, you will notice that there have been some very interesting postscripts to the many stories told. Stainless Piping Materials would be another such postscript. I had been in my business for a number of years when Bert Warshaw took ill. His company began to suffer, and, before long, it was in major financial trouble. The bank took over and the company was up for sale. By now, I was doing very well and an out-of-town competitor was getting ready to buy Stainless Piping Materials. I did not want that to happen and outbid the competitor. I had not been to the Humboldt Park offices in many years but now I owned the company, the company where I had started out. Though the staff had all left, I found a note left for me on the company blackboard. It was written by Bert's daughter. It read: "Congratulations, Alfy. Things have really come around full circle." Eventually, I would close the office, for there was really no compelling reason to keep it open. I had bought the inventory and acquired the name. It was a reminder of where I had started and how far I had come.

Of course, success did not happen overnight. Perhaps the easiest business decision I would make in all of my years in business was determining the name of my venture. What should I call this new company? I decided on Sharon Piping and Equipment. Why Sharon? It was the name of my oldest grandchild, Rena's daughter. It brought me a lot of joy to name the company after her. It was also to bring me plenty of luck. I should add that the Sharon that I am speaking about was little more than a toddler when I made the decision to name the company after her. She is now a full fledged judge, serving in the military court system of the Israel Defense Forces.

You may wonder how it was, after readily admitting that I had little money nor access to much, that I managed to raise enough to begin my business. I figured that I should go to people who knew me. I went to my kibbutz and borrowed $15,000. Of course, I greatly appreciated it, but besides helping me, it had an interest in my success. It saw in Sharon Piping and Equipment the opportunity to sell Habonim valves. I also had a friend, someone who had great confidence and trust in me, who lent me another $15,000. He was a businessman and saw it as a business proposition. All I could offer him in return was 50% of the business which at the time was still 50% of nothing. After several years, I bought him out. How did his investment turn out? He walked away with $80,000. Not a bad return and a lot better than your average CD.

What did I do with the money? I found the cheapest and smallest space that would serve my needs. It was in Rosemont, a suburb of Chicago that was adjacent to the airport. It was small and I was running a bootstrapped operation, to put it mildly. I could not afford shelving at the beginning so my inventory was on the floor. I could not afford much for heat, so I kept the temperature very low to save money. It was not too comfortable and I still remember Yael and Alex, who were visiting me at the time, huddled up against the air vents trying to keep warm.

I used the rest for working capital and began searching for orders. I had some contacts with import brokers and it did not take me long to start getting some orders, but, if my timing had been good until then, it would take a turn for the worse in those first few months. There was a strike by dockworkers on the east coast and the equipment that I had imported was being diverted elsewhere which did me no good. I felt that since I had made commitments to my customers and had given them my word, I had to come through with what I had promised. What should I do? I bought from my competitors, selling at a loss to my customers. Looking at things from the long-term, it seemed like the only thing to do.

A one-man operation by day, the nights would be spent with Lil working away. We would eat dinner and then gather around the dinner table to do all of the administrative work. She would work all day at her business and then work with me, often until well past midnight, sometimes until two or three in the morning. We did all of the paperwork, everything that I did not want to do during the day so I could maximize my time selling. I figured if we could survive the stress of that first year or so, we would be okay. Once some cash came in, one of the first things we did was to hire our first employee. I was now not just my own boss; I now had an employee to worry about. It really made a difference. The fellow whom I hired was a bit limited, but he did a fine job of handling the inside sales. It allowed me to get out of the office and on the road so I could see customers. We then hired two women to work in the office.

Lil was doing all of the payroll. Her mother was a bookkeeper and she had helped Lil with learning some of the rudiments of the trade. Although she would eventually cut back her hours at Sharon Piping, she continued to do the payroll for a fairly long time until we were able to hire internal staff to handle it. Even Sherry was doing some work, helping with the correspondence between our office and the manufacturers in the Far East.

There are many different approaches to take in business. A number of years ago, I was visiting a man at his office in New York City, high above the Manhattan skyline. He was a tremendously successful businessman. I suppose one might even have called him something of a tycoon. He was telling me about all of the companies that he owned and I listened intently. I began to think about my own small operation and what a challenge it was just keeping up with all that was going on there. I asked this businessman how he was able to keep abreast of what was happening in his far-flung operations. He showed me sheets of paper and pointed to a screen on his computer. To him, business was all about numbers—all about the balance sheet. If he did not like how the numbers looked, he might sell the company or one of its divisions, or, if he saw another business whose numbers he liked, he might buy it. What products did he make? What services did he sell? They mattered little to him. It was all about the numbers. I got the distinct impression from the time that I spent with him that the people did not matter much to him. They were spending 40 or 50 hours a week toiling away at his company, but they were no more than numbers. Their families depended on the paychecks that the employees were earning but they seemed not to figure into the picture at all.

I took an almost opposite approach. I was not only interested in the workers, but in their families as well. I suppose this relates to the fact that I have always been tremendously interested in people. I am known to speak to all different kinds of people, whether they are waiters in restaurants, taxi drivers—nearly anyone with whom I interact. I am also a naturally inquisitive type. Simply put, people fascinate me, and when they worked for me I took my responsibilities to them very seriously, just as I wanted them to take their responsibilities to the company very seriously.

When Sharon Piping was growing, we began to hire more and more people. Our head count at its peak was somewhere around ninety people. When you factor in spouses and children, we are talking here about a few hundred people. The thing that gave me the most pride about Sharon Piping was not its financial performance, not even its product performance, but, rather, its human performance for it was that human performance which led to the other two. Having my own company allowed me, as Frank Sinatra would say, "to do it my way." In fact, I was so identified with that song, that it was played at my birthday party. Part of doing things the Alfy Nathan way was giving people a second chance in life. One of our best workers in the warehouse was a man who had served time in prison. He was something of a model employee: very conscientious and a good family man. He turned his life around and found religion. It was very inspirational to see such a man at work. He realized that the only person who could bring himself out of the abyss was himself. Obviously, he did not have the greatest background in the world, but he wasn't looking to blame society. It was immensely gratifying to see that we could play a role in such a turnaround.

I have always felt that you can never help people enough. We are all in this thing together. When I say this thing, I mean life itself. Certainly, when I was on the kibbutz, that was the nature of how we did things, but it can be argued, I think, that you can do more for people through capitalism than you can through socialism. Our company was living proof of that. As we began to expand, we set up branch offices, in Memphis, Tennessee; Columbia, South Carolina; Houston, Texas; Avon, Massachusetts; and Los Angeles, California in addition to our Illinois location. We were interested in serving particular industries like oil and natural gas or a geographical area that had been underserved like New England. I had hired a fellow whom I met and was impressed with to be a branch manager of one of the locations. There was just one problem. He was a recovering alcoholic, but I felt that he was sufficiently committed to not drinking to give him the chance. Well, once when I was visiting the office, I smelled liquor on his breath and found that he had been drinking. He would go on benders and be away for a day or two, and no one would know where he was. Lil and I got to know his wife and tried to do everything possible to help, but ultimately I had to let him go. It was a sad tale. The man had ability and wanted to turn his life in the right direction, but his demons ultimately did him in.

People in the office were always encouraged to advance their careers by taking courses. We have paid for quite a few college and business-related courses. I wanted people to aspire to more and more. I wanted to reward them fairly for their efforts. It gave me pleasure when I looked out in the parking lot one day to see that one of the salesmen had bought himself a new car, or when one of the folks in the office had made a down payment on a new home. Perhaps what gave me the greatest pleasure was seeing their families grow. The children were getting on, being graduated from school, going to work, and getting married themselves.

It could be said that I can be a bit paternalistic but I hope it is not in a bad way. I was always concerned to see my workers outside smoking. Well, you may ask that for someone who is against smoking, how was it that I was handling cigarette cartons in 1945? Well, first of all, it was the war, the circumstances were extreme, and the cigarettes were currency. People did not know that smoking was bad for them. By the time I was in business, there were warning labels on every pack of cigarettes. I knew that it was very difficult for people to quit so I thought I would give them a financial incentive. I would tell people that if they stopped smoking for so many months, I would write them a check for $400.00. You would be surprised by how many people turned me down. Money does not motivate everyone but I felt I had an obligation in certain areas. Sometimes employees sought my advice. I tried to help wherever I could even if it was just to listen and be a sympathetic ear.

Chicago is a very diverse city and our workforce over time reflected this diversity. We had many workers who were Hispanic, black, Irish, Italian, and Polish. In a certain sense, it is reminiscent of what I said earlier about Israel: the challenge of mixing different elements and getting them to work together. For such a combination, people seemed to get on quite well. It is amazing how business (this is why I am a big believer in capitalism) helps blur the differences that exist between people of different skin colors, religions, and nationalities. We had people stay for 10, 15, 20, and 25 years. I remember when we had a party for an employee's 25th anniversary. How many people spend 25 years at a company these days? We must have been doing something right.

If you know me, you may have gathered that I am not crazy about unions. I am not alone among business owners in that respect. Let me qualify my distaste for them, however, by stating that I not only believe that at one time unions were necessary, I think they were essential. They did many good things for the working person. Over time, the unions got very powerful and began hurting both business and the workers they claimed to represent. They take money from worker's paychecks, try to coerce their votes in political elections, and otherwise are a pain in the neck to the entire economy.

What would have happened if a union had gotten its tentacles around Sharon Piping? Thank God it never happened, but why did they never try? That our company was spread out in six states, several having right-to-work laws in place, probably helped fend off any offensive on the part of the unions. Why was I so negative about unions? A bitter taste still resonated from my days in Israel where the Histadrut ran the show. I don't know that I would have continued being in business if I had to deal with a union. While a union would have been bad for Alfy Nathan, the real victims would have been the workers themselves. The only ones who would have made money on the deal would have been the union officials.

The first business that I worked in was H. Nathan, my father's clothing store. Though we had outside employees, it was still primarily a family business. I had never perceived that Sharon Piping would have a family element to it but I was pleasantly surprised when that occurred. My brother, Barry, had been working for an Israeli company when he was sent on a contract assignment to Sri Lanka. The timing was not good because not long after he arrived, a civil war broke out, an on-again off-again affair that would last for nearly twenty-six years, ending only in 2009. Barry could not stay in the country and was weighing his options. He called me from Sri Lanka and I told him that he should come to Chicago to work for Sharon Piping. He agreed and came to Chicago with his wife, Lottie.

Barry was a tremendous asset to the company, helping organize many functions in the office and helping keep our costs under control. Barry is a fine person who is hard working and very respectful of other people. He became quite popular not just among our staff, but with everyone with whom he dealt. He had a very positive impact on the company. Lil and I appreciated having Barry and Lottie in town and it was a unique opportunity to spend time with them. He was able to get a green card, something that he assures me today would not be possible. I knew they were unlikely to stay permanently, but they stayed for fifteen years. Barry and Lottie always intended to return to Israel because of their children and grandchildren, so he retired from Sharon Piping and lives happily with Lottie in Haifa.

At around the same time that Barry called me from Sri Lanka, I had a conversation with my son-in-law, Alex Winkler, who, after marrying Yael, had spent seven years living on the kibbutz, working for Habonim. He was doing well working there, learning many of the facets of the business, just as I had years earlier. It is very hard to adjust to life on the kibbutz if you have lived elsewhere, especially if it is somewhere like the beaches of Tel Aviv which are so very different from the kibbutz. Alex was definitely interested in a change and his parents had long since left Israel and were living in Vancouver. He and Yael came to Chicago and Alex began a successful career with our company, culminating with his taking over the valve division, of which he is currently president.

One of the nice things about having Alex around is that it gave me the opportunity to bounce ideas off someone. He is a very sharp fellow and full of ideas, always looking to the next product. As on the kibbutz, we were not very big on formality. Many of our meetings, at which major decisions were made, were held at a local eatery. We would discuss a strategy or a competitive challenge and, hopefully, by our second cup of coffee, or at worse, our third, we'd come up with the right solution.

While I had left the kibbutz, I was still doing plenty of business with the kibbutz, but I found that not all of their product lines were suitable. I could beat their prices by importing from the Orient. I should make it clear that at Sharon Piping we did not manufacture anything. We would import parts and then assemble the final product, whether valve, actuator, or fitting from them. That is not to say that we did not have anything proprietary. We had our own line of valves called Sharpe which was an acronym of Sharon Piping and Equipment. Barry came up with the name and it stuck, developing an excellent reputation in the field.

We were importing from Asia and if you look at where we imported from, you can get a bit of a lesson in imports over the last thirty years. First, we were bringing in products from Japan; then it was Korea, Taiwan, Malaysia, and, finally, China. Like all businesspeople, I was searching for the cheapest prices which also meant the least expensive labor. I suppose I was no different from the Jewish farmer whom we encountered in Hadera who wanted to use only Arab labor. Of course, the quality had to be there. To ensure that it was, I traveled to Asia nearly once a year. Lil often escorted me on those trips and some were quite memorable.

When most people travel to Japan, it is usually to the big cities, which are generally equipped with Western style hotels. We went to the city of Hanamaki, far enough north in the country that it had ski slopes. There we stayed in a Japanese hotel which meant that you slept on the floor, on mats. Well, we had quite a time getting up, and, if you guessed that there was no cable television in the room, you would be correct. There was a communal bath in the hotel, but we decided to take a pass. If the hotel sounds a bit ancient to us Westerners, the factory was very high-tech, with a robot, which seemed right out of a science fiction movie, doing more than its share of the work.

If the accommodations took some getting used to in northern Japan, we would have no such problem getting acclimated when we were invited by our Japanese hosts to Singapore for an opening of a new factory. We were put up at their expense at a very posh hotel that left an orchid on our pillow every night. We went with our Japanese hosts to visit a museum that had an exhibit about the Japanese surrender there. Initially, the Japanese had led an invasion of Singapore, and though many of them were on bicycles and faced a larger British force, they defeated the British. It is considered among the worst military defeats in British history, and much of the exhibit that we saw dealt with the

Japanese treatment of the prisoners of war and the civilian population. As you can well imagine, it was not very positive. The Japanese were tremendously cruel and thousands died from a variety of causes. It was hard to believe that the Japanese with whom we dealt, whose courtesy and gentleness was beyond belief, could be capable of such barbarism. It showed us how much had changed since the war.

We took a fascinating trip to Korea. When not doing business, we had a tour guide take us around. The one place we shall long remember was the border between North and South Korea, the most heavily guarded border in the world. It is a very tense place and it makes our old border with the Syrians look relatively relaxed. There were loudspeakers coming from the North Korean side, inviting their countrymen in the south to come join their worker's paradise. Very few have taken them up on their invitation.

Back on the home front, there were changes that forced us to reconfigure our setup. By the 1990s, the freight industry had changed dramatically. United Parcel Service could deliver very speedily and at reasonable cost. The other shipping companies followed suit and domestic shipping became quite inexpensive. It made us rethink the wisdom of having five warehouses all over the country. They were no longer cost effective. We decided to shut down South Carolina, California, Texas, and Massachusetts, keeping our location in place in Memphis. This also cut down my time on the road, which, as I got older, took some burden off of me.

Sharon Piping had come a long way. We bought out another competitor who had fallen on hard times and were soon seen as an industry leader. Despite our growth, I did not want us to get too large. I had seen enough examples of where companies had grown too large too quickly to know how to avoid this pitfall. One of our great advantages was that we could turn around orders very rapidly. We had the inventory on the shelf and could get it out much faster than many of our competitors. This was a big help. Of course, we still needed cash to expand. Besides inventory, we had gone from our original 3,500

Standing in the warehouse of Sharon Piping.

square feet in Rosemont to 10,000 square feet in Northlake, and then expanded there to 17,000 feet before moving to our current location which housed our entire operation and was 37,000 square feet. I had lines of credit that allowed for such expansion, but I never forgot the meeting I had with a local banker in the early years. Though I had little in the way of collateral, he lent me a sizable sum. I asked him why he did it. He told me that he had taken a trip to the warehouse and had seen it was a busy place. His gut told him to take a chance on me and he did. Today, with increased regulations and computer modeling, he would not be able to make such a loan.

The opening of our new building was accompanied by a big shindig. We invited customers and friends, and though you never want to take success for granted, I suppose it was a moment that represented the fulfillment of my dream. Lil had placed flowers in all the fittings and everything looked spectacular. Of course, when the excitement died down, it was time to get back to work.

CHAPTER TWELVE

Looking Forward

We had been living in Glenview for a good number of years, and though we were happy in our home, as we were getting older we thought that a ranch (single-story) house might make our lives a bit easier. After looking around, we found a house that was to our liking. The only problem was that it needed some work. In fact it required a complete remodel. Searching the yellow pages for an appropriate candidate to do the work, I got to the letter "C" and saw an advertisement for Clark Construction.

When Lil and I met Marty Clark, we were both surprised at how young he was. He was still in his twenties, having worked his way through college and was now operating his own construction company. We discussed a remodel with him and after hearing us out, he suggested that we consider building a new home. After talking it over, it was clear that building from scratch was the way to go. We found a piece of property in Northbrook that we liked. We bought it and tore down the house that stood there. The back of the property looked out at the county's nature preserve, no one could build there, and that was one of its major selling points.

Marty did a beautiful job and we were extremely pleased with the house when we moved in December of 1994. We became quite friendly with Marty and were impressed with not only his work but his character. He was an immigrant who had come from the Middle East; thus the two of us had much in common. Marty's family came from Iraq. They were Assyrians, an ancient Christian people who had suffered greatly from Muslim persecution. After his parents divorced, when the children were young, his mother made her way from Iraq to Lebanon in a covert way that would have done Mossad LeAliyah Bet proud. She eventually came to Chicago, which had a large Assyrian community.

Like so many immigrants, Marty had a strong work ethic and was full of ambition. We decided after our home had been built that we should become partners in building homes. Each party would have their role. Marty would do the work and we would provide the investment capital, splitting the profits. Our goal was to build similar homes to ours, large, comfortable residences on the north shore of Chicago. Our home would serve as a model and we were so trusting of Marty that we gave him a key so he could feel comfortable to show our home to potential buyers.

We built the homes on speculation but had no trouble selling them. In fact, Marty built fifteen in five years and we were profiting from the partnership in ways that were not strictly financial. I enjoyed watching the progress of each home, would drive by and watch the workmen. I also enjoyed watching the success of a young man. Marty was a very family-oriented fellow. He involved one of his sisters in the business. He also bought a beautiful colonial home for his mother where he built an office from which she could run her dressmaking business.

Marty seemed to be on top of the world, buying a boat, in which he would take people out, loving the opportunity to entertain friends and relatives. He became more than a friend or a partner. He became a member of the Nathan family, joining us for family simchas and holidays, buying Lil beautiful gifts for her birthday. Then one day, he got up and did not feel well, so much so that he went straight to the hospital. After some tests, they found nothing and told him to go home. Apparently, they indicated to him that nothing was wrong. But something was very, very wrong. Soon, Marty returned to the hospital and this time the tests were conclusive. It was everyone's worst nightmare: cancer. He went for treatments, but nothing seemed to work. He was going steadily downhill, becoming weaker and weaker. We went to visit him frequently in the hospital and before long, he was in hospice care.

Within six months of the diagnosis, Marty had passed away, thirty two years young. Both Lil and I had felt like we had lost a family member. We did our best to comfort his mother and sisters, but, as you can imagine, this was not easy. About four years after Marty had passed away, we received a visit from one of his sisters. She handed us a check and when we asked her what it was for she explained that Marty had kept a certain sum of money in escrow for each home that he built. This was in the event that something went wrong with one of the homes and the money stayed in escrow for four years after construction of the home. When he knew he was going to pass away, he had instructed his sister to hold the money for the specified period and then write us a check for 50% of the amount. That was Marty, his sense of honesty continuing even after he had passed from this earth. It was a lesson to all of us.

When I married Lil, I told her there was one condition; we would have to visit Israel on a regular basis. Well, she was more than agreeable. As the business became more successful, we increased our travel. These were not just for enjoyment's sake alone. The challenge of blending a family together was considerable and we both knew it was important to work at it. To give our children and grandchildren the opportunity to get to know each other, we arranged trips and eventually took cruises together. While we could not force anyone to forge a close relationship, we wanted to give them ample opportunity to

Here are 31 of the very smartly dressed Nathan clan, enjoying our Alaskan cruise together in August 2008. Inset: Our 3 grandchildren who were unable to attend.

Family vacations with our children.

bridge whatever culture gaps that might exist. These vacations were very special to us and we considered them essential for building family harmony.

The holidays were a major focus of our family, just as they had been when I was growing up. Passover and the Passover Seder was a point of emphasis for us. One of the reasons that we built a large home was that we wanted to be able to accommodate not only our relatives but many friends as well. It was not unusual to have 30–40 people for the Seder. I mentioned in a previous chapter that the Seders on the kibbutz incorporated the traditional Haggadah with modern themes from Jewish history. I very much liked this concept and set out to put out an Alfy Nathan style Haggadah. I had always felt that the young people were bored at the Seder and felt that they needed to be energized with more contemporary themes. So I brought in the Holocaust, the state of Israel, Soviet Jewry, things that seemed to be relevant. I

Photo from the Tribune article about the Nathan Passover.

Photo by Peggy Wolff

also included agricultural themes and some of my experiences on the kibbutz. Apparently, word of the Nathan Haggadah spread and a freelance writer, Peggy Wolff, shortly before Passover in 1989, decided to write an article about it. The article appeared in the Sunday Chicago Tribune and everyone seemed to rather enjoy it. Alfy Nathan was now a celebrity. Fortunately, it did not go to my head.

Though I believed in making certain innovations with the Nathan Haggadah, I loved the traditional Haggadah and all that it represented. I particularly enjoyed the wise saying of our Talmudic sages, which make up a significant portion of the beginning of the Haggadah. I say beginning to emphasis those parts that are read before we get down to the business of eating the meal, which everyone seems to rather fancy. These sayings I had learned as a boy, listening to my father conduct the seder in the manner that he had learned it from his father, and on and on, an unbroken chain that goes back to the very Exodus itself.

One saying that I remember is one that is read soon after the youngest child has recited the four questions, and right before we get to the four sons. Some say the story in question dates from the time of the Bar Kohkba revolt, when the Jews stood up to the mighty Roman Empire 1,875 years ago. (It was the last time an independent Jewish state existed in the Land of Israel until the modern state was formed in 1948.) As it goes, five rabbis were sitting around in B'nei Brak, expounded on some of the finer points of the Exodus when Rabbi Eleazar Ben Azariah says, "Behold I am like a man of seventy years old. . . ." Apparently, this statement is taken from the Talmud and Rabbi Eleazer Ben Azariah was not a man of seventy at all but rather was a very young man of eighteen when he was appointed to a very high position, not usual for someone of such youth, so he uses the word "like."

Seventy is an important age, for in addition to being the age of a wise old man, it is considered the natural lifespan of a person, derived, many say from the life of King David. I was well past that age and approaching my 82nd birthday when a thought popped into my head. A custom has developed to have a second Bar Mitzvah at the age of

83, considered to be a great milestone but really it was just a matter of simple math. 70 + 13= 83. Since my first Bar Mitzvah had been so difficult due to the untimely death of my mother, the idea of going through a second ceremony very much appealed to me. (And I was not even looking for presents.) Since we were members of Congregation Beth Shalom in Northbrook, I went to see Rabbi Wolkin and ran the idea past him. Though the synagogue had never held a second Bar Mitzvah before, he warmed to the idea.

It was important to both Lil and me that I have my Bar Mitzvah on a Shabbat when no other Bar or Bat Mitzvah was scheduled. We did not want to take attention away from a thirteen year old. In a synagogue with over 1,000 families, this was not easy to pull off but we secured a date. Of course, there was one thing I had to do, learn the Haftorah portion. This would be challenging enough but as luck would have it, it turned out to be an especially long Haftorah. At 82 years young, it would take me a bit longer than the average thirteen year old to learn it. Fortunately, I had a wonderful teacher, Susan Stoehr, the wife of our cantor, Steven Stoehr. She was very patient and worked with me for the better part of a year, coming to the house and helping me with the proper way to sing the trope and pronounce the words, neither of which were easy.

By now you have figured out that Alfy Nathan, like Frank Sinatra, does things his way. In keeping with my image, I had one more request to make of our rabbi. It is standard practice for the Bar Mitzvah boy, in addition to thanking everyone who helped him, to speak about the Torah portion of the week or the Haftorah reading that accompanies it. Just as in the Nathan Haggadah, I wanted to give the ceremony a more contemporary feel and therefore asked if I could veer a little bit from the typical speech. Rabbi Wolkin must have believed that I could add something unique and so he gave me the go ahead. I got up in front of the 200 or so assembled in the sanctuary and spoke about Operation Magic Carpet, also known as Operation on Eagles Wings, the exodus which brought Jews not from Egypt but from the country known as Yemen. In doing so, I returned to an earlier time in my life, to 1949 and 1950 when 47,000 Jews were airlifted into Israel. I still remember seeing those weary Yemenite faces soon after they stepped on to Jewish soil. I spoke a little about the Yemenites in an earlier chapter and about the tremendous culture shock that they had to endure. As you can tell, these memories have stayed with me these last 60 years. I thought the congregation, particularly the younger folks who may not have been aware of this event, would benefit from hearing about it. Judging by their reaction, they did.

After the service, the 200 or so in attendance, some regular parishioners, some friends and relatives, were all invited to a wonderful repast. Wow, was it something! Many remarked that the Nathan kiddush was one the best that they had ever been to. For making it so wonderful, as in so many of the other joyous events in my life, I have my lovely wife, Lil, to thank.

I started my own business at a later age than most people. Starting the company in my 50s, I was now well into my 80s when a major decision could no longer be put off. It is a decision that every business owner is faced with at one time or another. It involves the future of his business and what is the best way to execute what is called an "exit strategy." One of the most common of such strategies is to sell the business. Not that every owner who sells had pre-determined that course of action beforehand. Sometimes he is not even thinking of selling. There are times that he may be approached by a competitor or other interested party and the offer is to good to turn down. In my case, I had made the decision to sell. I had put off retirement for a long time, having been blessed with good health. But I knew it was time to slow down a bit and enjoy life and my family a good deal more. The inevitable had arrived and I reasoned it was time to act.

I spoke in the introduction of this book about the importance of hiring a professional. I was not going to try and sell Sharon Piping myself. I found a business broker who came highly recommended and seemed to have a good track record selling industrial oriented companies. I was sufficiently impressed upon meeting him and decided to retain him. He learned about the business and after accumulating the financial data, sent out a prospectus to potential buyers. If they were interested, they needed to sign the usual confidentiality agreement. Until there was genuine interest on the part of a perspective buyer, the identity of our company was hidden. There was response from about thirty entities. Not bad. Some were in our area or a related field. Some were investment companies who were interested in the company as a pure financial investment. At each stage of the bidding process, the numbers of suitors were getting smaller and the dollar figures were getting larger. Finally, we were down to just a couple of bidders.

Sharon Piping was an attractive company for a number of reasons. We had a very clean balance sheet, were not saddled with much debt and had few liabilities. We had a good reputation and solid management in place, even the CEO was not half bad. Our product line was unlikely to be made obsolete with technological innovation. We were so attractive in fact, that I was genuinely amazed at the level of interest. Our timing was also good, in that the financial markets were peaking in 2007.

Secrets are hard to keep and the greatest fear in any prospective sale is that employees will find out what is going on and begin to wonder about their future. I tried to be honest and upfront. Of course, I was planning on taking care of my people, not only making sure they stayed on after I had sold, but paying some key people a bonus from the proceeds of the sale. Who bought Sharon Piping? Remember Ron Kersten from Los Angeles, the fellow who wanted me to join him as a partner nearly thirty years earlier. We stayed in touch over the years and he was one of the bidders and eventually bought the company, merging it with his operation. I was very happy with the price that we got for the company, but like so many other things in life, I had mixed emotions about parting with a business that I had started and, like a child, had seen grow to maturity.

The valve business was the big draw for Ron and the company is largely unchanged today. Alex runs the valve operation and most of the employees have remained. The company has weathered the hard economic times fairly well but since Ron sold 50% to a private equity group years ago, things are a bit different. Decisions are no longer made over a cold drink and a sandwich as they were when I used to work with Alex. Now, there are board meetings, and board members to contend with. The buyer had insisted that I stay on in a limited role for a two year period to ensure a smooth transition. I worked ten hours a month and I will not tell you my hourly rate but can assure you that it was considerably more than I made when picking Jaffa oranges sixty years earlier. Now the two year period has passed and Lil and I spend the winter months in Florida with so many of our fellow retirees.

Looking forward is the name of this, the final chapter of the book. It is not the final chapter of Alfy, though. There really is much to look forward to. Seeing our children become grandparents as our grandchildren become parents is very exciting and a privilege that not all get to enjoy. We try and keep our minds and bodies active. We take courses in Florida, go to museums and concerts for the mind and spirit and walk for exercise. We spend time with our many longtime friends and find that we find that we are never too old to make new ones. People still fascinate me and I am still trying to figure out what they are all about, still asking questions and still darned curious about all that encompasses life in this world. Though we live comfortably, what we most cherish is that our success has meant that we are in a position to do for others, to continue to participate in what is one of the central tenets of the Jewish religion since its beginnings, the obligation of charitable giving.

If the past is any indication of what the future will bring, I can honestly say that I never expect my life to be boring. Nor should the reader. The young reader, people like my grandchildren and great grandchildren may read this book and say, "Yeah, Grandpa Alfy's life was exciting but mine is so different." They may even think that it seems a little slow or boring in comparison to mine. But the truth is that the world is a very different place than when I was their age. Sure, there have been plenty of changes, some for the worse, a lot for the better. But you must never be afraid to go out there and meet challenges. You must never be afraid of an adventure, a new experience.

Adventure, by the way, does not have to mean being in the middle of a war. I pray that my grandchildren and great grandchildren never experience that, but adventure is challenging yourself every day to do a little more to make yourself better. It frequently entails small things. It may be school work, it may be a job, it may be a sport or a hobby, it may be a relationship. The bottom line is: don't be afraid to push yourself. Don't be afraid of failure. Things may not always work out the way you planned them, you may even stumble a bit. But I will tell you this much. My life was an "incredible life story" because I never stopped trying, never tired of striving and I always was interested in so much more than just Alfy. If you are honest, hard working, decent, caring, and manage to maintain a sense of humor in the face of all that comes at you, the "incredible" part of your life story will take care of itself. Take my word for it.

The two of us